RECONSIDERING CRIMINAL JUSTICE & LAW ENFORCEMENT:

Practices, Policies, and Paradigms

Dr. Gene Ira Katz, DMCJ

innovativeink
PUBLISHING
A Division of Kendall Hunt

Cover image © Shutterstock.com

www.innovativeinkpublishing.com
Send all inquiries to:
4050 Westmark Drive
Dubuque, IA 52004-1840

Print ISBN: 979-8-3851-2565-4
Ebook ISBN: 979-8-38751-2566-1

Published in the United States of America

Contents

Preface

The fields of criminal justice, law enforcement, and the practices, policies and paradigms related to these topics, contain a wide range of issues that can hardly all be contained in a single volume. This book is intended to present an overarching sense of the trends, range, and reach of various professional perspectives and behaviors that tend to affect individuals, and society in general, whether or not one is directly involved with policing or the criminal justice system.

The collection of essays presented here reflect doctoral-level research in subject matter and style, meaning that each piece is substantiated by extant data and is crafted at the highest level of academic exposition. While selectivity was exercised in determining which facts to incorporate and which to exclude, leading to an emphasis of certain perspectives and the omission of others, it's important to note that these are not editorial pieces, while acknowledging that some readers may sense the promotion of particular viewpoints over others. The intention here is to foster further discussion concerning important issues that may be overlooked, misunderstood, or controversial to an extent that they seem to resist more thorough discussion.

That being stated, several recurrent themes have played a guiding role in shaping the overall content. These encompass a dedication to societal inclusion and diversity, transcending class, race, or ethnicity; a steadfast commitment to the equitable administration of justice; and a strong emphasis on evidence-based methods, and evidence-based policing, which refer to policies and professional behaviors proven to be the most effective according to the scientific method, existing research, and best practices as defined through the most authoritative sources related to the fields covered here.

This book is not meant to be the final word on any of the issues presented here, but rather is intended to inspire continuing inquiry, especially on the part of legal, law enforcement and legislative professionals who drive the practices, policies, and paradigms in our criminal justice system.

Some of the material in this book was previously published in *American Police Beat, Law Enforcement Today*, and *The US-China Law Review.*

The author acknowledges several colleagues for their support in completing this collection of essays, including Dr. Jaime Sampayo, Dr. Tina Bynum, Dr. John Gidduck, Dr. Reo Leslie, Dr. James Thorpe, Ms. Molly Brewton, and Chief (Retd) Dave Edmond.

1

Law Enforcement Management Concepts for Enhancing Diversity

a katz/Shutterstock.com

Introduction

This paper presents some ideas for implementing a program on training criminal justice organization managers to enhance their management skills, organization function, and processes, thereby enhancing the success of their respective organizations, especially insofar as addressing changing demographics within their ranks and the communities in which they serve. This will include some discussion about cultural, legal and other factors that could serve as obstacles to such innovations, as well as how to implement these improved approaches.

Law enforcement agencies fulfill a fundamental role in our society, and in many communities individual police officers are often the public face of local government. It therefore is critical that our nation's law enforcement agencies broadly reflect the diversity of the communities they serve.[1]

Conventional wisdom would seem to suggest that more proportionate and representational ethnic and racial diversity in America's police departments would have a positive effect on police/community relations. This idea was emphasized in the Final Report of the President's Task Force on 21st Century Policing, an extensive exploration of relevant issues launched by President Obama and finalized in 2015, as exemplified by this quote from the report: "law enforcement agencies should strive to create a workforce that encompasses a broad range of diversity including race, gender, language, life experience, and cultural background to improve understanding and effectiveness in dealing with all communities."[2]

In December 2015, the U.S. Department of Justice's (DOJ) Civil Rights Division and the Equal Employment Opportunity Commission (EEOC) undertook an extensive research project called "Advancing Diversity in Law Enforcement," in order to identify obstacles that thwart diversity in America's police forces, and to draw attention to encouraging practices that are likely to facilitate agencies in better reflecting the diversity of the communities in which they serve. This initiative primarily concentrated on obstacles and promising processes in three central areas: recruitment, hiring, and retention. In so doing, this project has taken an in depth look at numerous barriers to diversity, while also addressing favorable practices that are likely to promote greater racial and gender diversity, and also encouraging the perspectives and knowledge of persons with diverse backgrounds in the culture and leadership of law enforcement agencies.[3]

It should be noted that one of the presenting problems throughout the U.S. hindering full implementation of the "Advancing Diversity in Law Enforcement" program is that communities with widely culturally diverse populations have had considerable difficulties in recruiting enough new law enforcement personnel to represent minority residents at a proportional level, as represented by the chart in **Figure 1** below.

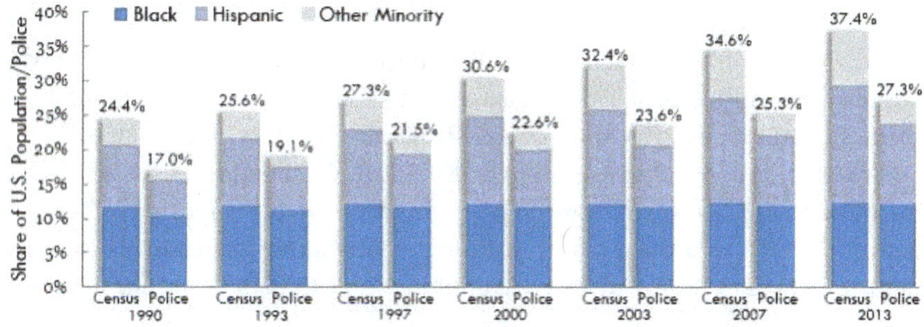

FIGURES REPRESENT NATIONAL TOTALS FOR MORE THAN 12,000 LOCAL POLICE DEPARTMENTS IN THE BJS SURVEY
SOURCES: BJS LEMAS SURVEY, U.S. CENSUS BUREAU POPULATION ESTIMATES PROGRAM

How the Strategy Is Organized and Implemented

The first step in implementing the kind of changes advocated in the "Advancing Diversity in Law Enforcement" program is to ensure that a law agency's organizational culture is guided by community policing, as described in the aforementioned President's Task Force on 21st Century Policing, which can be simply described as a strategy of policing that focuses on police building ties and working closely with community members. In addition, the agency must adhere to the concepts of procedural justice, which is the idea of employing fairness in the processes that resolve disputes. Finally, the agency must also fully embrace cultural inclusivity, which welcomes and includes all kinds of people, regardless of race, ethnicity, place of origin, gender or orientation.[4]

As they embark upon a program of expanded diversity, the law enforcement organization must be willing to interact with all interested parties, both from inside and outside the agency, in order to help create a workforce that reflects the diversity of the community. They must also be willing to re-evaluate their usual employment criteria, standards, and objectives - to make sure that they are fitting to the talents required to perform job tasks - and are thereby able to attract, select, and retain the most qualified and suitable officers.[5]

These are some of the steps that the DOJ has identified as boosting the recruiting, hiring, and retention of diverse applicants.

RECRUITMENT:

Proactive and purposeful outreach will tend to encourage people from diverse populations within the agency's jurisdiction to consider careers in law enforcement. Effectively using technology and social media will help to communicate and reach out to the entire community. Establishing affiliations with educational institutions and offering internship programs for students will help establish an active roster of potential recruits, while at the same time helping to address any negative perceptions that diverse communities may have of the police.

HIRING:

Law enforcement agencies shown to be the most successful in diversity hiring are increasingly embracing a more inclusive perspective about what talents and assets that applicants can offer to the organization. Among other issues, this also means a willingness to reconsider information revealed during background checks, such as previous drug use, minor arrests, and so forth.

Agencies must be willing to reconsider selection benchmarks, and written or physical assessments, that do not directly correspond to job-related duties, and that therefore excessively wind up excluding applicants from underrepresented populations. Another means of attracting more diversity among applicants is to streamline and bring more transparency to the hiring and selection processes. For instance, some organizations provide help and preparation materials to assist applicants in preparing for examinations, while others have invited community members to become more directly involved in the hiring process in order to develop a police force that reflects the diversity in their localities.

RETENTION:

Apprenticeship programs which partner up veteran officers with rookies, as well as leadership training, are recognized as critical in providing newer officers with the kinds of encouragement and guidance they will require to thrive on the job, to appreciate their career choices, and to earn promotions, and these kinds of programs are especially useful for those from underrepresented populations

Community collaborations and ongoing engagement with various civic and merchant groups can be very effective in helping to retain officers of color and women by providing them, as well as law enforcement leaders, with a fuller perspective of the particular challenges they may face in their profession. This can also help lead to providing additional resources to fund incentives, such as providing temporary housing, enabling officers to work towards college credit while on the job, or offering financial bonuses for language skills. These kind of programs have been shown to help retain officers with diverse experiences and backgrounds.[6]

How the Strategy is Sound and Effective

Diversity within law enforcement agencies is defined not only in terms of race and gender, but also other characteristics including religion, sexual orientation, gender identity, language ability, cultural background, and experience. Police forces that reflect this kind of diversity are seen as a vital part of building and maintaining trust within communities in which they serve. These findings are supported by substantial research confirming that when members of the public perceive their law enforcement organizations as representing, understanding, and responding to them, and when authorities are generally seen as being fair, genuine, and accountable, it significantly improves trust in the police, while also supporting the public's confidence in government. The data also strongly indicates that increased diversity can make law enforcement agencies more amenable to reform, more willing to initiate cultural and systemic changes, and more responsive to the individuals in the communities they serve.[7]

Federal Laws Relevant to This Problem

According to the U.S. Equal Employment Opportunity Commission (EEOC), the agency responsible for enforcing federal hiring laws:

> It is illegal to discriminate against a job applicant or an employee because of the person's race, color, religion, sex (including pregnancy, gender identity, and sexual orientation), national origin, age (40 or older), disability or genetic information. It is also illegal to discriminate against a person because the person complained about discrimination, filed a charge of discrimination, or participated in an employment discrimination investigation or lawsuit.[8]

Some Impediments in the Development and Implementation of the Strategy

The history of previous attempts at police reform, including increased diversity, are filled with stories of well-intentioned and highly publicized planned changes, and assurances of dramatic transformations, but many of those promises faded away over time, with either minimal or no impact. Many citizens have come to believe that America's police are unwilling or unable to reform themselves, and moreover, that police culture is resistant to all efforts toward their accountability. Even a cursory review of police history tends to support to this very pessimistic view.[9]

More recently, another potential impediment to implementing law enforcement management diversity strategies has emerged. For years national law enforcement agencies have been sounding the alarm about white supremacists infiltrating their ranks. In 2006, the F.B.I. issued a report warning of white supremacists plans to join police departments and to recruit like-minded officers. In 2009, the Department of Homeland Security issued their own report informing the public and local law enforcement of the significant threat to national security posed by white supremacists after the election of Barack Obama, America's first black president. Both agencies have issued comparable updates since, backed up by similar reports from organizations such as the Anti-Defamation League (ADL), the American Civil Liberties Union (ACLU), and the Southern Poverty Law Center (SPLC). In the time that has passed since the first of these warnings, there has been an alarming number of police officers reported to be members of hate groups or expressing racist vitriol in texts, emails, and on social media.[10]

It should also be noted here that shortly after the President's Task Force on 21st Century Policing was published, a report was released by the Legal and Liability Risk Management Institute (LLRMI), a nationwide organization of legal and professional consultants on matters of public safety and criminal justice procedures. Their report challenges whether communities do experience positive effects with improvements in diversity recruitments for police departments, with substantial evidence that communities of color do not show African-American officers any more respect. In fact, comprehensive research on this matter reveals that African-American police officers tend to be treated worse than white officers when dealing with African-American citizens, and quite a number of studies with African-American law enforcement officers have revealed that they encounter more hostility and resistance from citizens of all races than do white officers.

These kinds of counterintuitive results show up again and again in the literature, strongly suggesting that simply increasing ethic integration is not necessarily a solution to improved police/community relations.[11]

Conclusion

The DOJ and the EEOC have generated many documents tracing the increasing efforts of many law enforcement agencies to improving recruitment from the diverse cultures, ethnicities and races in their localities, and they have provided a plethora of materials to assist any police organizations who want to do the same. The blueprints for such endeavors are available, and the pathways are clearly laid out. It seems the primary impediments are not in the abilities to make improvements in hiring new recruits from diverse populations, but in the willingness and sincere intentions of law enforcement leaders to follow through and get it done.

ENDNOTES

1. DOJ, 2016.
2. DOJ, 2015.
3. DOJ, 2016.
4. DOJ, 2016.
5. DOJ, 2016.
6. DOJ, 2016.
7. DOJ, 2016.
8. EEOC, n.d..
9. Cohen, 2017.
10. Johnson, 2017.
11. Johnson, 2015.

REFERENCES

Cohen, R., (2017), The force and the resistance: Why changing the police force is neither inevitable, nor impossible. Retrieved from https://scholarship.law.upenn.edu/cgi/viewcontent.cgi?article=1207&context=jlasc

Johnson, R.R., (2015), Police-minority relations: What should be done? Retrieved from https://www.llrmi.com/articles/legal_update/2015_johnson_minorityrelations/

Johnson, V.B., (2017) The epidemic of white supremacist police. https://theappeal.org/the-epidemic-of-white-supremacist-police-4992cb7ad97a/

U.S. Department of Justice [DOJ]/Equal Employment Opportunity Commission[EEOC], (2016), Advancing Diversity in Law Enforcement. Retrieved from https://www.eeoc.gov/eeoc/interagency/police-diversity-report.cfm

U.S. Department of Justice, (2015), Final Report of the President's Task Force on 21st Century Policing. Retrieved from https://cops.usdoj.gov/pdf/taskforce/taskforce_finalreport.pdf.

U.S. Equal Employment Opportunity Commission, (n.d.), About EEOC. Retrieved from https://www.eeoc.gov/eeoc/

2

The Expanding Militarization of US Law Enforcement

Darleine Heitman/Shutterstock.com

Introduction

Over the past half century, under the auspices of the federal government, most of the 18,000+ police forces across the United States have increasingly acquired military grade weaponry, equipment and personal armor. In addition, especially following the terrorist attacks of 9/11, many of the law enforcement agencies have embraced combat style training, while also establishing specialized squads that enforce the law as though they were soldiers on an assault mission. What follows provides detailed information on the reasons for this trend, some of the attempts to reign it in, and a comprehensive strategy to limit the continued militarization of America's police, based upon the collected insights of knowledgeable authorities in the fields of criminal justice, law enforcement and civil rights.

The Militarization of America's Police

The literature on the subject generally agrees that the militarization of police in the U.S. began during the mid-1960s with the creation of the first SWAT, or Special Weapons Attack Team, by the Los Angeles Police Department (LAPD) in their effort to combat the dramatic proliferation of well-armed urban youth gangs, and the pervasive increase in violent street crimes overall. The SWAT members underwent military style combat training, were armed with submachine guns, and were deployed to crime scenes in armored vehicles. After a number of striking successes, particularly the apprehension of a heavily armed unit of the Black Panthers in 1969, and the highly publicized take down of the Symbionese Liberation Army in 1973, famous for kidnapping heiress Patty Hearst, police departments across the nation took notice, and soon thereafter well over half of all U.S. cities with populations of 50,000 and above created their own SWAT units.[1]

In 1989, Section 1033 of the National Defense Authorization Act allowed the U.S. Secretary of Defense to provide surplus military equipment to state and local law enforcement organizations, with the intention being to improve efficiency and safety during anti-drug and counterterrorism operations.[2]

While there was a significant drop in violent crime across the U.S. through the 1990s funding, support and enthusiasm for SWAT units took a downturn as well.[3] However, following the terrorist attacks on 9/11, the U.S. Congress enthusiastically promoted wide distribution of available military equipment in support of homeland security across the nation, and the face of America's police forces transformed as never before, as departments large and small became tasked with protecting the citizenry from a new and frightening menace that seemed to be invisible and everywhere at once.[4]

In a 2011 edition of *The Atlantic*, U.S. Department of Justice analyst Arthur Rizer, a former Washington State police officer and decorated U.S. Army veteran of the Iraq War, collaborated with lawyer and Georgetown University PhD Joseph Hartman, in a report entitled "How the War on Terror Has Militarized the Police." The authors note that as the first line of defense again terrorist attacks on American soil, police departments of all sizes across the country had significantly expanded their employment of military-grade materials and weaponry, including a complete range of equipment from body armor to attack helicopters. Quoting from their report,

> Police departments have employed their newly acquired military weaponry not only to combat terrorism but also for everyday patrolling... Now, police officers routinely walk the beat armed with assault rifles and garbed in black full-battle uniforms... In recent years, police departments both large and small have acquired bazookas, machine guns, and even armored vehicles (mini-tanks) for use in domestic police work.[5]

The report also notes that, as mentioned earlier, in the beginning only the largest American cities had SWAT teams, and they were used only when extraordinary force was required, while today almost every police department in the country has at least one SWAT unit, many of them trained by special forces commandos, and all too often they are deployed for relatively minor operations, search as serving warrants, and even wellness checks.[6]

Addressing Various Factors That Have Caused the Increase in Police Force Militarization

While a significant increase in urban street crime was one of the primary causal factors that started the militarization of America's police in the contemporary era,[7] and the events of 9/11 accelerated the already expansive 1033 Program,[8] there are several additional causal factors that are essential in in order to understand and address the current ubiquitous presence of militarized law enforcement across the U.S.

Causal Factors

The wide variety of military grade equipment that has been increasingly acquired by U.S. law enforcement agencies, both large and small, is available through a number of different federal agencies, not just the Department of Defense (DOD), but also through the Department of Justice (DOJ), the Department of Homeland Security (DHS), the Treasury Department, Department of Interior (DOI), the General Services Administration (GSA), the Defense Logistics Agency (DLA), and the Office of National Drug Control Policy (ONDCP).[9,10]

While every one of the recipient police departments are supposed to report all of the military equipment they have acquired to the DOJ, only the DOD keeps track of which agencies have received which equipment from them, which means that there is no comprehensive tally of who has what. In addition, once a law enforcement agency has possession of the military equipment, they are considered the owners, and as such are able to trade or lease those materials to other agencies. Again, none of this is tracked by any federal regulatory organization.[11]

Adding to the problem of this lack of transparency as to which police departments own which military gear, the American Civil Liberties Union (ACLU) reports that even the General Accountability Office (GAO), an independent, nonpartisan agency which examines how taxpayer dollars are spent, often called the "congressional watchdog," has long complained that the DOD, which is the only agency that tracks equipment acquisition, does not verify the identities of the individuals who take possession of materials, nor are the quantities of items recorded. Their records indicated that some private security firms, even non-existent agencies, have acquired military grade weaponry through the 1033 program.[12]

Another causal factor that needs to be addressed is the proliferation of brokers within the federal government, such as the DLA Disposition Services, who actively solicit police departments, including federal, tribal, state, and local law enforcement agencies, to become owners of any kind of military grade equipment that would otherwise wind up warehoused or on the scrap heap.[13]

Another major factor to be addressed is the influence such militarization has had upon police culture across the U.S. Sarah Lustbader, criminal defense attorney and former senior program associate at the Vera Institute of Justice, and Vaidya Gullapalli, senior legal counsel at the Justice Collaborative, reported on an extensive 2018 Stanford University study of 9,000 U.S. law enforcement agencies, published in the Proceedings of the National Academies of Sciences, said to be the first systematic analysis on the use and consequences of militarized force. Among the findings: many police agency supervisors consider SWAT teams and other militarized units necessary for police and public safety, while in reality, as mentioned earlier, in the majority of cases they are routinely used for drug busts and serving arrest warrants. One disturbing trend was revealled wherein SWAT teams were much more likely to be used in predominantly Black neighborhoods. As part of the study, hundreds of open records requests were sent to agencies, but most of them do not track militarized operations, and those that do keep inadequate records, refuse to share, erase them over time, severely redact them, or demand extremely high payments for anyone seeking to acquire them.[14]

Another less extensive, but still substantial study, was presented in a Law Enforcement Bulletin for the FBI by State University of N.Y., Buffalo, Criminal Justice Department's Associate Professor Scott W. Phillips. Of the 370 agencies surveyed, from small departments of less than 25 officers, to those above 500, the results were generally consistent regardless of the agency's size. One finding indicated that "police agencies will not shy away from using the (SWAT) teams for incidents they see as potentially dangerous," and "70 percent of the leaders answered that deployment practices would not change for a protest or civil unrest."[15] A majority of respondents did not consider it necessary to make changes in the use of black or camouflage uniforms, armored SWAT vehicles, or carrying military style rifles, despite the widespread acknowledgement that for the most part, the public sees the militarized appearance as unacceptable.[16]

These findings, combined with the aforementioned Stanford study, strongly indicate that police culture, regardless of the agency's size, has come to identify with the more militarized style, which has increasingly inculcated their ranks since that first L.A. SWAT team came on the scene in the late 1960s. In short, police forces throughout America have been stockpiling easily accessible military equipment with practically no accountability, while embracing military style training, and increasingly assuming a soldier's mentality. In so doing, contemporary police have been transforming the characteristics of peace officers into those of soldiers.[17]

Addressing the Causal Factors

Following from the section above, there are certain challenges that are required in order to address the causal factors related to the increased militarization of America's police. Among them is the development of procedures to limit the availability and range of military grade equipment that law enforcement agencies may acquire. Another would be the transparent, precise and comprehensive accounting of what equipment has been transferred, for what purpose, and to whom. Perhaps the most difficult challenge of all would be a nationwide refutation of the acceptability and opaque nature of the transformation of America's police departments from community peace-keepers and protectors, to what are essentially paramilitary platoons occupying the town square.

Prior Actions Taken to Limit the Increased Use of Military Assets by U.S. Police

What follows are some real-world applications of existing programs that reflect the objectives and potential for enacting limitations to police militarization.

While President Obama decided to significantly limit access to the DOD's 1033 Program in 2014 following the extreme show of military might by the Ferguson police department during the riots that followed the Michael Brown shooting, in 2107 President Trump authorized an expansion of the program to its former robust accessibility for U.S. law enforcement agencies.[18] However, a few individual states have attempted to address some of the problems associated with police militarization. In 2009 Maryland enacted a short-lived law requiring every police agency in the state to record their SWAT activity in a uniform, transparent manner, following a botched raid on a local mayor's home from faulty information that resulted in terrorizing his family and the death of his dogs.[19] In 2015, the state of New Jersey, enacted a law that required municipal and county law enforcement agencies to receive approval from local legislative bodies before obtaining military equipment. In 2015 Montana enacted a law restricting state and local police from obtaining certain military equipment from the 1033 Program, such as weaponized drones, aircraft configured for combat, grenade launchers, silencers, and militarized armored vehicles. Police must also issue a public notice 14 days before requesting any military grade equipment, and they may not use any grant funding for purchase of 1033 materials.[20]

These partial attempts to limit access to military equipment, or to require more accountability, represent potential steps that could go much further, perhaps to the point of mandating approval by state or local legislators for all acquisitions, along with complete transparency in reporting the rationale for the obtaining the equipment, and reasons for its employment.

Campaign Zero is a citizen activist group that seeks to reform some of the most egregious behavior of America's police personnel. They regularly report on state level progress toward demilitarization, such as detailing over 107 recent laws addressing police violence, and how at least 10 states have passed legislation commensurate with Campaign Zero's agenda. Their proposed measures to demilitarize involves a number of practical action steps, similar to some of those already mentioned, but much more expansive. At the top of their list is to do away with the 1033 Program altogether, which would require Congressional legislation.

This organization has also targeted adjacent behaviors that promote and support military style actions, such as no-knock arrests without probable cause.[21]

Campaign Zero is not the only organization challenging the status quo. In the wake of President Trump's rejuvenation of the 1033 Program, an extensive coalition of over five dozen civil liberties and public policy organizations signed open letters to Congressional leadership urging a halt to the program, as well as for hearings to be conducted about its usefulness. This coalition included the ACLU, the National Association of Criminal Defense Lawyers, The Constitution Project, FreedomWorks, the NAACP, the Law Enforcement Action Partnership, and numerous other groups from the left, right and in between, that all expressed opposition about the need for these weapons of war in domestic law enforcement.[22]

Two more issues to address in order for an innovative strategy to limit the increased use of military assets by U.S. police to be successful must be included, and those are officer accountability and the redress of harm resulting from these oversized and extreme tactics. G. H. Reynolds, Beauchamp Brogan Distinguished Professor of Law at the University of Tennessee explored the problem in a 2014 article entitled "SWAT Overkill: The Danger of a Paramilitary Police Force." He asserts that all police raids should be recorded on video, in a tamperproof format, and that police who break-in to the wrong house, or who have not given sufficient notice, aside from actual life-or-death circumstances, should not be allowed the cover of official, so-called 'qualified immunity', often afforded to sworn officers by prosecutors. This would include filing charges against officers for using flash-bang grenades and other extreme, disorienting tactics, which may force the homeowner to think they are being invaded by intruders, and attack back to protect their home and family. Such homeowners will almost always face charges, but seldom will the invading officers.[23]

Limiting the Increased Use of Military Assets by U.S. Police

Limiting the increased use of military assets by U.S. police would require the intentions, impetus and participation of a number of key players, not the least of which would be the chiefs and supervisory leadership of each department, as well as local, state and federal lawmakers, in addition to federal regulators and agency administrators, as will be detailed further on. For such a strategy to work, there must be oversight, restrictions, and clearly expressed reasoning for the acquisition of any military grade equipment, in addition to transparency in its use, the maintenance of a complete inventory, and specific location of each item. There also needs to be a clear set of guidelines adhered to as to when, and if, any of this equipment is to be used, if at all.

Referencing the 2015 President's Task Force on 21st Century Policing would be an obvious starting place to begin formulating a strategy to limit the increased militarization of America's police, as it presents extensive descriptions on the purpose and characteristics of Community Policing, which emphasizes proactive collaborations and partnerships between local law enforcement and the civilian population [see Chapter 17].[24] Routine use of SWAT and displays of military equipment are antithetical to the highly interactive "cop on the beat," conversational style inherent to Community Policing. It should be noted that resistance to Community Policing across America has been widely documented,[25] although millions of dollars have been distributed by the DOJ's Community Oriented Policing Services (COPS) to over 80% of U.S. police departments (COPS, n.d.), many of whom barely enact the full set of steps required for true Community Policing.[26] Without belaboring this piece of the strategy here, the DOJ document, "Community Policing Defined," clearly details how localities can adopt and employ this effective challenge to more militarization of local police and the funding for embarking on such a course of action is readily available from the COPS program, as mentioned.[27]

A central, 501(c)3 clearinghouse could be created, along the lines of Campaign Zero, or the Southern Poverty Law Center (SPLC), perhaps headquartered in Washington, D.C., with local outposts established in every state. The executive staff for such an organization would consist of concerned veteran law enforcement leadership personnel, authoritative jurists, and criminal justice professionals, along with current and former lawmakers, all of whom would be committed to dramatically reducing the militarization trend. This clearinghouse would provide up-to-date information on emerging militarization incidents, as well as guidance for citizen-based and legislative actions. This clearinghouse would collect and curate expertise and advisory alerts from the 60 plus civil liberties and public policy organizations that signed the open letters to Congressional leadership urging a halt to the 1033 Program, as mentioned above. However, rather than a one-time partnership, this would be an ongoing collaborative action, where the aim would be to create concrete results, targeting every local, state, and federal law enforcement agency that routinely deploys military grade equipment and that presents officers as though they are combat ready soldiers. The clearinghouse would spearhead lobbying for legislation at all levels of government that would urge transparency and accountability for all SWAT activities, such as perpetually recording such events with tamper-proof police-cams, and not allowing police to continue to be protected by inordinately broad immunity policies for law enforcement personnel.

Another aim of this clearinghouse would be to maintain contact with police academies across the U.S., and the American universities with major graduate programs in Law Enforcement in order to promote an anti-militarization agenda, and provide guidance, expertise, learning materials and presentations, particularly targeting cadets and students who are interested in going into supervisory and leadership occupations in policing. In-service trainings for active police force supervisors would also be promoted.

Finally, the clearinghouse would launch and maintain an ongoing, highly visible, public advertising campaign, similar to the Partnership for a Drug Free America- "This is your mind on Drugs",[28] to promote the anti-militarization message, utilizing every mass-media available, including web ads on the internet and across all social-media, plus television, radio, print ads, billboards, etc. A consistent set of anti-militarization communications would present the issue in simple stark terms, as represented in the example provided in **Figure 1**.

Figure 1
Source: Public Domain

Conclusion

Although, over the past half century, numerous police departments across the U.S., large and small, have acquired and regularly use military grade equipment, weaponry and outerwear, and this trend has been dramatically increasing since the 9/11 terrorist attacks, there has also been an increased groundswell among knowledgeable leaders, academics, lawmakers, civil rights activists, and criminal justice authorities who want to see this trend curtailed and reversed. Some attempts have been made to reign in the militarization, as mentioned above, but except for a few stand-alone civic minded organizations, there has yet to be a robust, country-wide effort to address this issue head-on, as a national problem that needs to be confronted and remedied.

The concepts presented in the clearinghouse strategy described above would go a long way to force a national dialog at the highest levels of power, as the literature clearly indicates that America's citizenry is overwhelmingly opposed to having their hometown police presented as an occupying military platoon of enforcers, rather than as protectors and service providers, along with the tragic loss of life and limb that have all too often accompanied this growing and dangerous trend. Once there is a highly vocal groundswell of popular opinion on this matter, positive changes will eventually manifest, through the power of the ballot and control of the public purse strings.

ENDNOTES

1. Rivas, 2013.
2. Phillips, 2017.
3. Lind & Lopez, 2015.
4. Phillips, 2017.
5. Rizer & Hartman, 2011.
6. Rizer & Hartman, 2011.
7. Rivas, 2013.
8. Phillips, 2017.
9. Executive Office of the President, 2014.
10. Wofford, 2015.
11. Wofford, 2015.
12. Bennett, 2017.
13. DLA Disposition Services, n.d.
14. Lustbader & Gullapalli, 2018.
15. Phillips, 2017.
16. Phillips, 2017
17. Rizer & Hartman, 2011.
18. Clark, 2017.
19. Barry, 2015.
20. Vyse, 2017.
21. Campaign Zero, 2020.
22. Blanks, 2017.
23. Reynolds, 2014.
24. DOJ, 2015.
25. Lurigio & Skogan, 2016.
26. Lurigio & Skogan, 2016.
27. DOJ, 2014.
28. Philanthropy News Digest, 2005.

REFERENCES

Barry, D., (2015), Stop the war on Baltimore. Retrieved from https://www.thenation.com/article/archive/stop-war-baltimore/

Bennett, T., (2017), Even fake law enforcement agencies can get weapons of war for 'policing.' Retrieved from https://www.aclu.org/blog/criminal-law-reform/even-fake-law-enforcement-agencies-can-get-weapons-war-policing

Blanks, J., (2017), An open letter to rethink 1033. Retrieved from https://www.cato.org/blog/open-letter-rethink-1033

Campaign Zero, (2020), Demilitarization. Retrieved from https://www.joincampaignzero.org/demilitarization

Clark, D., (2017), Trump makes it easier for police to get military equipment. Retrieved from https://www.nbcnews.com/politics/white-house/trump-makes-it-easier-police-get-military-equipment-n815766

DLA Disposition Services, (n.d.), Join the 1033 Program. Retrieved from https://www.dla.mil/DispositionServices/Offers/Reutilization/LawEnforcement/JoinTheProgram.aspx

Executive Office of the President, (2014) Review: Federal support for local law enforcement equipment acquisition. Retrieved from https://obamawhitehouse.archives.gov/sites/default/files/docs/federal_support_for_local_law_enforcement_equipment_acquisition.pdf

Lind, D., Lopez, G., (2015), 16 theories for why crime plummeted in the US. Retrieved from https://www.vox.com/2015/2/13/8032231/crime-drop

Lurigio, A.J., Skogan, W.G., (2016), Winning the hearts and minds of police officers: An assessment of staff perceptions of community policing ion Chicago. Retrieved from http://wechargegenocide.org/wp-content/uploads/2016/07/crime+delinquency.pdf

Philanthropy News Digest, (2005), Partnership for a Drug-Free America. Retrieved from https://philanthropynewsdigest.org/npo-spotlight/partnership-for-a-drug-free-america

Phillips, S.W., (2017), Police Militarization. Retrieved from https://leb.fbi.gov/articles/featured-articles/police-militarization

Reynolds, G. H., (2014), SWAT overkill: The danger of a paramilitary police force. Retrieved from http://www.popularmechanics.com/technology/military/4203345

Rivas, J., (2013), Militarization of the police force: Causes and the alternative. Retrieved from https://digitalcommons.calpoly.edu/cgi/viewcontent.cgi?article=1129&context=socssp

Rizer, A., Hartman, J., 2011, How the War on Terror Has Militarized the Police. Retrieved from https://www.theatlantic.com/national/archive/2011/11/how-the-war-on-terror-has-militarized-the-police/248047/

U.S. Department of Justice, (2014), Community Policing Defined. Retrieved from https://cops.usdoj.gov/RIC/Publications/cops-p157-pub.pdf

U.S. Department of Justice, (2015), Final Report of the President's Task Force on 21st Century Policing. Retrieved from https://cops.usdoj.gov/pdf/taskforce/taskforce_finalreport.pdf

Vyse, G., (2017), Trump wants to re-militarize the police. Montana is having none of it. Retrieved from https://newrepublic.com/article/144600/trump-wants-re-militarize-police-montana-none-it

Wofford, T., (2015), Tanks for nothing: Why Obama's plan to end police militarization may be dead in the water. Retrieved from https://www.newsweek.com/2015/06/19/battle-get-americas-police-part-their-military-gear-340949.html

3

More Effective Trends in Law Enforcement Training

photo from: cops.usdoj.gov/sixth-annual-attorney-generals-award-distinguished-service-community-policing

Introduction

This chapter presents the background and development of police training in general, and then discusses some of the aspects required to create effective programs for training criminal justice organization leaders, to better enhance leadership skills, which then promotes the success of their organizations. Factors such as key players, economic implications, as well as ramifications regarding political, legal, and organizational culture, will be addressed, among other issues related to successful and unsuccessful leadership techniques and skills within contemporary criminal justice organizations, along with some of the difficulties and challenges that such leaders currently face.

Background and Brief History of Police Training

The first official police force in the United States was formed in Boston, MA, in 1838, followed over the next two decades by New York City, Chicago, Cincinnati, New Orleans and Philadelphia. By the late 19th Century most communities had some type of police force.[1] Policing in the U.S. is conventionally broken into three historical eras [see chapter 7], the Political or Traditional Era, from 1890 -1930, when law enforcement officers were generally seen as following the directives of local political bosses, and working closely with the people in the neighborhoods in which they served; the Reform Era, from 1930-1980, which introduced the widespread use of scientific findings and technology to policing; and the Community Era, from 1980 – the present, which ushered in the promotion of expanded cultural sensitivity, collaboration with civilian entities, and closer engagement with the individuals served by the local police force. Some believe that a fourth, Homeland Security Era, began in the wake of the 9/11 terror attacks, which has yet to be universally accepted by law enforcement scholars.[2]

Early on, and throughout the Political Era, almost all officers patrolled on foot or by bicycle, prior to the widespread use of the automobile, and officer training occurred informally on the job.[3] New recruits were generally paired up with more seasoned officers, and they learned their professional skills through direct experiences, accompanied by the seasoned advice of their seniors. This would most likely have been the only training any police officers, up to and including department chiefs, would ever have had during the first era of policing.[4]

The first formal training academy devoted to police work was established in 1908 at the University of California, Berkeley, by that city's police chief, August Vollmer, considered by many to be the Father of American Policing.[5] Vollmer, who served as Berkeley's Chief Marshal, and later chief of the Los Angeles police force, was widely known for "professionalizing" his own departments, as well as numerous other police agencies across the nation, and internationally. Vollmer has been credited as the creator of the polygraph machine, radio patrol cars, and the first crime lab in America. It would be fair to say that Vollmer was ahead of the times, and in large part was responsible for ushering in the Reform era of policing, which emphasized science and technology, as well as formal training for all police officers.[6]

Early in the Reform Era, a 1935 article, "Police Training--Its Needs and Problems," by George H. Brereton, Deputy Director for California's Department of

Justice, asserted the necessity for the establishment of educational standards and training for police which are comparable to those found in many other professions. In his article, Brereton, in turn, quoted Donald C. Stone, founder of the American Public Works Association, who also strongly promoted the need for officer training, stating that "so broad are the problems with which the police must deal that to learn police work entirely through experience would require a lifetime or more...Why should a man learn the criminal law through trial and error, if he can learn it through instruction?"[7]

Effective Police Officer and Law Enforcement Leadership Training

In 1923, August Vollmer issued a statement expounding what he thought were the seven most important points of police training: 1) high educational, mental, moral and physical standards for all recruits; 2) psychological assessments for all recruits during the training period; 3) withhold exercise of police authority until the new recruit shows by conduct and comprehnsion that they are fit for such service; 4) preparatory and promotional courses should be available for officers in colleges and universities; 5) establish crime prevention divisions and appoint trained criminologists to lead these division; 6) establish a merit system for promotions; 7) educate the public and invite their friendship and cooperation with the local law enforcement agency.[8] With that last step Volmer foreshadowed the essence of modern Community Policing, over a half century earlier, and his forward-thinking guidance has come to be realized in the preponderance of contemporary police training as well.

A 1959 piece by Honolulu's police chief, Daniel S.C. Liu, entitled "Professional Standards of the Police Service," stated that "the qualities of integrity, honesty, justice, decency, benevolence, compassion, and all the other virtues we look for in wholesome leadership throughout the world are the same qualities that we desire to see represented throughout all of the police service."[9]

The above wisdom from these formative authorities of the Reform Era reflect some of the fundamental issues related to the qualities required of leadership attributes in law enforcement today. While many comparisons have been made about similarities between supervisory training for both the military and police, Dr. Wes Doss, an experienced training instructor for both sectors, observes that the military places far more emphasis on advanced training and leadership development early in one's career than is typical in law enforcement. Military leaders receive the training before assuming the supervisory position, unlike in law enforcement where there is often little or no training for new supervisors or managers, or the training happens after the promotion.[10]

The University of San Diego's Academic Director of Law Enforcement and Public Safety Leadership, Erik Fritsvold, offers the elements that he believes are most essential for effective law enforcement leadership training. Topping the list are so called "soft skills," such as communication, team building, problem solving and conflict resolution, which are hardly ever developed sufficiently by most individuals without some kind of formal training. Other capabilities include understanding how to connect well with people from diverse backgrounds, often under stressful conditions, the capacity to collaborate with individuals and other agencies without having to 'be the boss,' and a solid sense of ethics and emotional intelligence, which is defined as handling interpersonal relationships judiciously and empathetically.[11]

The Law Enforcement and Public Safety Leadership program developed by Dr, Fritsvold incorporates topics such as media and community relations, techniques for successful community engagement, dispute and conflict resolution skills, and procedures for evaluating crime trends. Clearly, these types of subjects are in keeping with the spirit of Vollmer, Brereton, Liu and other progenitors of intelligent and effective policing skills. More recently, Fritsvold wrote "Today, many departments are beginning to recognize the benefits of a more inclusive, transformational approach, rather than relying solely on the more militaristic, authoritative approach that has characterized police work for so long." He also asserts that advanced education in the fields of law enforcement and criminal justice is common among the most effective police leaders.[12]

Less Effective Law Enforcement Leadership

As indicated, effective law enforcement leadership training starts with hiring recruits who are suitable for police work, and then providing the proper kind of training, as described by Vollmer, et al. According to the Bureau of Justice Statistics, 83% of all U.S. police departments require a high school diploma, while only 8% require a 4-year college degree,[13] but even those rank and file officers who lack in formal law enforcement education upon their recruitment could and should still obtain effective training, as described above.

There are some 18,000 federal, state, city, local and tribal law enforcement agencies in the U.S., each with its own rules and standards. This also means significant variations in factors such as organizational culture, sense of social responsibility, available funding, local statutes, and community relations, and more, all of which can impact the effectiveness, even the purpose, of leadership training.[14]

The Department of Justice (DOJ) investigation of the Ferguson, MO, police department, following the shooting of teenager Michael Brown in 2016, led to a consent decree that extensively overhauled the normal operating procedures of the local police department. Among other failures of law enforcement, the investigation revealed that the leadership of the Ferguson PD was closely overseen by the municipal courts and political leaders, with the primary goal being to earn income for the city coffers by imposing fines on Ferguson's citizens, particularly people of color. This is an example of ineffective leadership training, as actual police work was used to advance corruption and discrimination by the city leaders and magistrates.[15]

Similarly, the DOJ investigation of the Los Angeles Police Department's Rampart Division led to a 2001 consent decree forcing the LAPD, the nation's second largest municipal agency, to adhere to a strict set of DOJ guidelines, from the pursuit of street gangs to community relations to internal investigations. In this case, the failure of leadership involved turning a blind eye to the runaway violence and criminal activity among the officers of the Ramparts Division.[16] Had the LAPD leadership followed the basic tenets set forth by experts like Doss, Fritsvold, and Vollmer-- who once ran the LAPD--events such as the Ramparts scandal would probably have never occurred.

Emerging issues that currently challenge effective law enforcement leadership training may include handling the increase in mass shooting events, opioid addiction within normally non-criminal populations, ever-changing immigration policies, and human trafficking, among others. The proliferation of white supremacist recruits in rural police department, often hidden or easily overlooked by human resources personnel, is another growing challenge to effective leadership as motivations based upon hate supersede serving the law.[17] These, and other emerging issues, are either so recent, or so mutable, that effective training may be lagging behind.[18]

The Current State of Police Officer and Law Enforcement Leadership Training

According to the Census of Law Enforcement Training Academies (CLETA), there are over 600 state and local law enforcement training academies in the U.S.[19] In addition, over five dozen major U.S. colleges and universities also offer accredited programs in law enforcement and corrections, among them NYU, Oberlin, Penn State and UMass/Amherst.[20]

In recent years there has also been a proliferation of smaller universities and community colleges that offer various levels of law enforcement programs, from certificates, as well as Associates through Doctoral degrees, designed specifically for those seeking to become leaders in criminal justice organizations. One such school is Colorado Technical University, with about 21,000 students attending classes at two campuses, Aurora and Colorado Springs, as well as online. Their Master of Science degree program in Criminal Justice includes such courses as Criminology and Public Policy, Issues of Diversity in Criminal Justice, Applied Managerial Decision-Making and Law Enforcement Management, while their Doctor of Management in Criminal Justice includes Issues and Trends in Today's Criminal Justice Organizations, Diversity in Society and Criminal Justice, Criminal Justice Organization and Management, Ethics and the Criminal Justice Leader, Leadership Theory and Development, Strategic Thinking and Organizational Alignment, and other leadership intensive subjects.[21] This reflects the thoroughness with which even a smaller school can cover the steps of effective law enforcement leadership training, as well as underscoring the wisdom and influence of Vollmer and the others mentioned above.

Conclusion

The days of law enforcement leaders being able to simply learn on the job during their rookie years, and then move up the agency ladder to a supervisory position over time, are long gone. In a recent study, over 1,000 law enforcement supervisors ranked what they thought were the characteristics of effective and ineffective leaders. Effectiveness was overwhelmingly linked to integrity, work ethic, communication, and care for personnel, while ineffectual leaders were seen as lacking in these, and related traits. The study participants indicated that good leadership was achieved through a combination of training and education, experience, and accepting feedback from others. Interesting to note, the most highly-rated obstacle to effective leadership practices had nothing to do with budgetary problems, but those related to cultural, structural, and political difficulties.

ENDNOTES

1. Potter, 2013.
2. Bond, 2016.
3. Bond, 2016.
4. Brereton, 1961.
5. Bykov, 2014.
6. Oliver, 2017.
7. Brereton, 1961.
8. Brereton, 1961.
9. Liu, 1959.
10. Fritsvold, n.d.
11. Fritsvold, n.d.
12. Fritsvold, 2020.
13. MSNBC, 2014.
14. Debusmann, 2016.
15. Justice.gov, 2016.
16. Justice.gov, 2001.
17. Lennard, 2018.
18. Foster, 2018.
19. Bureau of Justice Statistics, 2013.
20. Maguire, 2019.
21. CTU, 2020.

REFERENCES

Bond, M. ,(2016), Eras in American policing. Retrieved from https://andragogytheory.com/2016/01/05/eras-in-american-policing/

Brereton, G.H., (1961) The importance of training and education in the professionalization of law enforcement. Retrieved from https://scholarlycommons.law.northwestern.edu/cgi/viewcontent.cgi?article=5013&context=jclc

Brereton, G.H., (1935), Police training--Its needs and problems. Retrieved from https://scholarlycommons.law.northwestern.edu/cgi/viewcontent.cgi?article=2557&context=jclc

Bureau of Justice Statistics, (n.d.), Law enforcement training academies. Retrieved from https://www.bjs.gov/index.cfm?ty=tp&tid=77

Bykov, O., (2014), Police academy training: An evaluation of the strengths and weaknesses of police academies. Retrieved from https://pdfs.semanticscholar.org/1109/442b13d5026b063e8ee5090839827189dd7e.pdf

Colorado Technical University, [CTU] (2020), Master of Science in Criminal Justice. Retrieved from https://www.coloradotech.edu/degrees/masters/criminal-justice/general.

Debusmannm B.,(2016), The race problem in black and white Retrieved from https://www.chathamhouse.org/publications/twt/race-problem-black-and-white

Foster, R.E., (2018), Top ten police management issues for 2018. Retrieved from https://www.mark43.com/top-ten-police-management-issues-for-2018/

Fritsvold, E., (n.d.), The case for more effective law enforcement leadership training. Retrieved from https://onlinedegrees.sandiego.edu/police-management-training/

Fritsvold, E., (2020), What style of police leadership is most effective? Retrieved from https://onlinedegrees.sandiego.edu/what-style-police-leadership-most-effective/

Justice.gov, (2016), Consent Decree. Retrieved from https://www.justice.gov/opa/file/833431/download

Justice.gov, (2001), Consent Decree. Retrieved from https://www.justice.gov/crt/us-v-city-los-angeles-consent-decree-introduction

Lennard, N., (2018), Even the FBI thinks police have links to white supremacists — but don't tell the New York Times. Retrieved from https://theintercept.com/2018/11/05/new-york-times-police-white-supremacy/

Liu, D.S.C., (1959) Professional standards of the police service. International Association of Chiefs of Police, Inc., 1959, pp. 169-170.

Maguire, A., (2019), The List of all U.S colleges with a law enforcement and correction major. Retrieved from https://blog.collegevine.com/the-list-of-all-u-s-colleges-with-a-law-enforcement-and-correction-major/

MSNBC, 2011, U.S. Police: Education levels and the use of force. Retrieved from https://www.msnbc.com/ronan-farrow-daily/us-police-education-levels-and-the-use-force-msna476106

Oliver, W. H., (2017), August Vollmer - The Father of American Policing. Retrieved from https://cap-press.com/books/isbn/9781611635591/August-Vollmer

Potter, G., (2013), The history of policing in the United States. Retrieved from https://plsonline.eku.edu/sites/plsonline.eku.edu/files/the-history-of-policing-in-us.pdf

4

A Community Oriented Approach to Law Enforcement

Steven J Hensley/Shutterstock.com

Introduction

We'll begin with a speculative scenario located in a fictional urban center called Cityville, population 650,000, where, after years of tough-on-crime, law and order conservative administrations, the voters have chosen to elect the considerably more liberal Mr. Mayor and Ms. Municipal Prosecutor, who have each promised what they have referred to as a "more humanitarian and compassionate approach" to law enforcement and criminal justice emphasizing, among other things, Community Policing, expanded opportunities for civilian involvement, improved communication and public relations, alternatives to incarceration where feasible, and vigorously upholding citizens' civil rights, with particular sensitivity toward those residents from ethnic minorities. What follows are some of the concrete, effective steps that may be taken in Cityville toward those ends.

Community Policing

The population of Cityville consists of a majority of white European descent, with about 30 percent representing non-white, Hispanic or Asian backgrounds. However, while in the minority, the arrest and incarceration rate for non-white citizens represents a disproportionately high number, with mathematical disparities estimated to be close to 40 percent above statistical probabilities, similar to the racial breakdown of arrest and conviction rates across the U.S.[1]

These distorted figures were frequently referenced by Mr. Mayor and Ms. Prosecutor during their campaigns, and both vowed to take significant action steps to correct these disparities and devote considerable resources and efforts to improve minority-culture awareness, involvement and sensitivity in Cityville, especially on the part of the municipal police force.

One premise promoted in the 2015 President's Task Force on 21st Century Policing report is that racially diverse police forces will improve understanding and effectiveness in dealing with all communities, although this argument is actually lacking support by almost all of the existing research evidence concerning this matter, which instead tends to report that communities of color do not show African-American officers any more respect, and, in fact, the research reveals that African-American police officers tend to be treated worse than white officers when dealing with African-American citizens.[2]

Despite these findings, Mr. Mayor chose to replace the former, hard line police chief with a younger, African American chief, along with a promise to increase recruitment of minority officers and to establish and promote Community Policing, which unlike increasing ethnic diversity in local law enforcement, has been proven by research to be a significantly positive factor in improving police-community relations.[3]

Community Policing has been hailed as "democracy in action," as it requires active sharing of responsibility through collaboration between local government, civic and business leaders, public and private agencies, non-profit/service providers, residents, religious organizations, schools, hospitals, local media, and everyone else who is concerned for safeguarding the welfare of the greater community.[4]

Community Policing is an attitude that promotes organizational policies to support efficient and methodical civilian/official collaborations for problem-solving, to preemptively address various conditions that lead to public safety issues, such as crime, social disorder, and collective fears about safety. Rather than primarily reacting to crimes only after they occur, Community Policing encourages law enforcement agencies, in partnership with community based groups, to develop solutions to identifiable conditions foundational to public safety problems [see Chapter 17].[5]

In Community Policing, the police department is no longer the exclusive enforcers of law and order, as all members of the community are encouraged to become actively involved in endeavors to improve public safety and the quality of life, not only in the commercial parts of town, but in even the most challenged of neighborhoods.[6]

In addition, Community Policing problem solving must be integral to police operations, not just catching criminals and enforcing statutes, and this solution oriented focus should guide all law enforcement decision-making. Officers must rethink making arrests as being only one of a variety of potential responses. Toward those ends, they are encouraged to utilize the SARA (Scanning, Analysis, Response and Assessment) crime problem solving model in coordination with all adjacent concerned agencies, as illustrated in the figure below:

Figure © 2024 Gene Ira Katz

Alternatives to Incarceration

Another concerted effort that Cityville's mayor and prosecutor are collaborating on is implementation of an expanded program of Alternatives to Incarceration (ATI), which are a set of sentencing choices available for prosecutors and judges meant to meet the standard goals of sentencing -- rehabilitation, punishment, and deterrence -- without relying upon costly, all-too-often unnecessary and counter-productive incarceration,[7] that, as mentioned, often disproportionately targets ethnic minorities, especially people of color.

Some of the most common ATI programs that have been adopted include Pretrial Diversion, which moves defendants from court proceedings and into a program designed to remedy the reasons for criminal behavior; Specialty Problem-Solving Courts, where defendants must attend regular individualized programs to address underlying issues that led to criminal behavior. Drug courts, mental health courts, community courts, domestic violence courts, re-entry courts, and sex-offense courts are all varieties of Specialty Problem Solving Courts. Community Corrections are another option, often operated by the local parole or probation office, where the defendants are required to attend general community supervision, day reporting facilities, halfway houses, work release, and other community programs.[8]

In locations with ATI programs, considerable cost-savings have also been realized. New York State, where about 160 such program are in operation, has seen a 17 percent reduction in incarceration since implementing these programs statewide, and in New York City, the incarceration reduction is over 40 percent. This totals over 20,000 less defendants behind bars across the state, with a cost saving of over $5,000 per prisoner, for over $1 billion of total savings via ATI.[9]

While Cityville may not experience such dramatic costs savings as these, ATI programs will likely significantly reduce court and incarcerations costs.

Improving Cultural Sensitivity and Relations with Minorities

In a Gallup poll nationwide, less than 50 percent of Hispanics and less than 35 percent of African-Americans believed that police officers would treat them fairly. As was alluded to earlier, arguably, the most frequently recommended remedy for this perception from civil rights groups, public officials, and law makers is to increase multicultural training for police officers and expanded diversification of law enforcement agencies by encouraging more recruitment from disadvantaged racial and ethnic minorities. While it may be argued that police departments should expand their ethnic and racial diversity because it is the right thing to do, research does not support the notion that such moves have done much to effectively improve relations between local law enforcement agencies and their minority citizens.[10]

Yale University Psychologist Elizabeth Paluck has put forth the idea that police agencies should cease offering classes in multicultural diversity and implicit bias training, and instead vigorously adopt programs that foster contact between groups from different cultural and racial groups. Her research indicates that whenever groups consisting of various racial, ethnic, gender, economic, and other different backgrounds, are obliged to collaborate collectively on a venture, or engage in recreational pursuits together, the prejudiced positions of those involved are substantially reduced, and remain so for an extended period of time after the joint undertaking. Psychologists from the University of California and Boston College examined over five hundred studies on such mixed group endeavors and their findings overwhelmingly support the assertion that such collaborations considerably decrease prejudicial opinions and conduct, and that those positive effects remain for months or years, strongly indicating that situations which bring law enforcement personnel and minority citizens together in partnership to address community problems, or situations where officers and minority citizens engage in joint recreational activities, can reduce prejudice and antagonism on both sides. Similarly, if officers would simply step out of their patrol cars with the intention of just conversing and getting to know minority civilians on their neighborhood beats, such down-to-earth interactions can also reduce negative preconceptions and antagonism for both the officers and the citizens.[11]

The Vera Institute of Justice, a national organization dedicated to building and improving justice systems that ensure fairness, promote safety, and strengthen communities, brings in experts to work with law enforcement agencies across the U.S. in order to foster what is referred to as bottom-up policing, where entire police agencies, not just special units or community liaisons, are listening to and collaborating with their communities. This kind of community-informed policing relies upon and upholds the relationship between public satisfaction and public safety, and seeks to employ alternatives to enforcement wherever possible.[12]

If Mr. Mayor is serious about improving the relationship between Cityville's police and minority residents, these kinds of attitudes and activities will go a long way toward achieving such ends.

Improved Police Communication and Public Relations

Police One.com, an authorative website for law enforcement personnel across the nation with over a million unique hits per month, provides well researched information and resources by experts in the field. Their 2019 article on media relations best-practices for police departments noted that an essential aspect for successful media relations from a law enforcement perspective is to establish active relationships throughout the community. They stated that, "The most important thing to do is be accessible and available."[13]

The National Criminal Justice Reference Service (NCJRS), advises police agencies who seek to improve community relations to establish a media relations unit, that is a department within the law enforcement organization solely responsible for handling communication with the news media and the public. This unit would be headed by either a civilian Public Information Officer (PIO) with a background in journalism and public relations, or by a police officer, who has some interest and training in media communication. The primary intention of the PIO is to establish official relations with news media personnel to better serve the community through ongoing education about policing practices and activities, as well as serving the interests of the police department, by establishing an enhanced position to shape the content of police-crime news and get ahead of "first-impression management" concerning how officer behavior is being portrayed in the media, particular in critical incidents [see Chapter 17].[14]

If Mr. Mayor is truly interested in improved police communication and public relations, he, along with the new chief, would do well to establish such a media unit and hire a knowledgeable and engaged PIO.

Potential Opportunities and Benefits from Civilian Overview

Civilian operated police review boards have been a controversial issue in the U.S. since first being introduce in the 1950s. An article posted in Governing, a breakout news operation from the Congressional Quarterly, and one of the most trusted and widely read sources on the subject of governance, noted that of 18,000 or so police departments in this country with formal officer oversight, in only about 200 or so does that oversight occur through civilian review boards, each with its own specific set of rules, responsibilities and procedures. However, such review boards often lack effectiveness and authority.[15]

Tim Lynch, director of the Cato Institute's Project on Criminal Justice, has examined civilian review boards across the U.S. and found that many are vulnerable to undue political maneuvering, insufficient funding and staffing, sluggish investigations and not enough authority or control to meaningfully investigate complaints.[16]

However, according to law enforcement veteran and author Olugbenga Ajilore, civilian review boards, when effective, uphold the reality of more even-handed and reasonable policing, by allowing non-police community members to observe and provide participation in police operations. Ajilore notes that appropriately empowered citizen oversight boards can increase and improve public cooperation and make communities safer for everyone.[17]

The key to their success, asserts Ajilore, is to be completely independent from law enforcement. "Boards need to have the authority to either discipline officers or recommend discipline of officers that department leaders will then enforce," he states. In addition, civilian review boards need sufficient funding and personnel to effectively oversee departmental activities.[18]

According to a report from the National Criminal Justice Reference Service, despite serious potential limitations, civilian police review boards have demonstrated some important benefits. Complainants have reported feeling validated when the board supports their allegations, or by having the opportunity to be heard by independent citizen investigators. They also felt that they were able to contribute to holding the departments accountable for police misbehavior. Even law enforcement personnel have reported some perceived benefits, such as an improved relationship and image within their community, and when the civilian board determines that the complaint was unwarranted, the public tends to feel reassured that the internal investigations of alleged officer misconduct has been thorough and fair.[19]

While there have surely been missteps and ineffective results in some of this nation's attempts at non-police review boards, Cityville could certainly increase civilian involvement and overview of the municipal police department by creating such an independent, citizen operated board, which would then tend to improve communication and understanding between law enforcement and civilians.

Some Concluding Thoughts

Cityville's new mayor and prosecutor both won in large part because of their promises to turn around widely held perceptions of an unfriendly police force that had reportedly been intimidating the ethnic minority population, while being uninvolved and removed from the day to day activities and characteristics of the various neighborhoods, and whose behavior was perceived to only emphasize punishment, and cracking-down on wrongdoers rather than engaging with the community humanely and fairly. Initiating the kind of steps outlined above, and additional similar forward thinking programs, these newly elected officials could go a long way toward accomplishing their stated goals for Cityville.

ENDNOTES

1. Langan, 1995.
2. Johnson, 2015.
3. COPS, n.d.
4. Gaffigan, 1994.
5. COPS, n.d.
6. Gaffigan, 1994.
7. LAC (Legal Action Center), 2019.
8. LAC (Legal Action Center), 2019..
9. Berman, 2013.
10. Johnson, 2015.
11. Johnson, 2015.
12. Vera Institute, 2019.
13. DeBlock, 2019.
14. Lovell, 2002.
15. Delgadillo, 2017.
16. Delgadillo, 2017.
17. Ajilore, 2018.
18. Ajilore, 2018.
19. Finn, 2001.

REFERENCES

Ajilore, 2018, How Civilian Boards Can Further Police Accountability and Improve Community Relations. Retrieved from https://scholars.org/brief/how-civilian-review-boards-can-further-police-accountability-and-improve-community-relations

Berman, G., (2013), Alternatives to incarceration are cutting prison numbers, costs and crime. Retrieved from https://for-ny.org/alternatives-incarceration-cutting-prison-numbers-costs-crime/

COPS-Community Oriented Policing Services/US DOJ), (n.d.), Community policing defined. Retrieved from https://cops.usdoj.gov/pdf/vets-to-cops/e030917193-cp-defined.pdf

DeBlock, C., (2019), Getting in front of the story: Media relations best practices for LE. Retrieved from https://www.policeone.com/media-relations/articles/483733006-Getting-in-front-of-the-story-Media-relations-best-practices-for-LE/

Delgadillo, N., (2017), Civilian oversight of police appeals to many, but is it always effective? Retrieved from https://www.governing.com/topics/public-justice-safety/gov-civilian-oversight-police-charter-amendment.html

Finn, P., (2001), Citizen review of police: Approaches and implementation. Retrieved from https://www.ncjrs.gov/pdffiles1/nij/184430.pdf

Gaffigan, S. J., et al., (1994) Understanding Community Policing. Retrieved from https://www.ncjrs.gov/pdffiles/commp.pdf

Johnson, R.R., (2015), Police-minority relations: What should be done? Retrieved from https://www.llrmi.com/articles/legal_update/2015_johnson_minorityrelations/

LAC (Legal Action Center), (2019) Alternatives to incarceration factsheet. Retrieved from https://lac.org/wp-content/uploads/2014/07/ATI_Factsheet.pdf

Langan, P.A., (1995) The racial disparity in U.S. drug arrests. Retrieved from https://www.bjs.gov/content/pub/pdf/rdusda.pdf

Lovell, J.S., (2002) , Media power & information control: A study of police organizations & media relations. Retrieved from https://www.ncjrs.gov/pdffiles1/nij/grants/197060.pdf

Vera Institute of Justice (2019) Building bridges between police and communities. Retrieved from https://www.vera.org/securing-equal-justice/building-bridges-between-police-and-communities

5

How Other Nations Address Cultural Diversity in their Criminal Justice Systems

NeydtStock/Shutterstock.com

Introduction

This chapter addresses some issues concerning the way countries outside of the U.S.A. deal with cultural diversity insofar as their criminal justice systems are concerned. Some of the topics covered will include unequal treatment of ethnic minority groups, the role of tribal, ethnic and multi-cultural traditions, attitudes toward women, girls and the LGBTQ+ population, along with similar related matters.

Considering Nations, Cultures and Identities

The United Nations lists 195 separate countries currently in existence.[1] The terms country, nation, and sovereign state may have slightly different meanings, depending upon the context and purpose in which each one of those words is used.[2]

For the objectives of this paper, each nation discussed will be considered as a **sovereign state**, meaning a distinct territory with internationally observed boundaries, with a population comprised of people living there on a permanent basis, and a recognized government with the powers to make treaties, form alliances, wage war, and create and enforce laws within its own independent domain.[3]

The term **culture**, as applied to a specified group of people, also has a wide variety of meanings, many of which include these generally understood concepts: shared knowledge accumulated over many generations, commonly held experiences, belief systems, philosophies, morals, viewpoints, and understandings about how one is to conduct themselves within the established hierarchy. Culture can also refer to a collectively held way of living, as well as a common language, symbolic meanings, and shared traditions.[4]

A related term, **ethnicity**, includes a group's cultural identity, and also relates to their common racial identity, religion, language, customs, or other particular qualities associated with that group.[5] **Racial identity** is closely associated with ethnicity, however, the concept of race relates specifically to physiological characteristics, including skin color, bone structure and other such features. Numerous modern researchers consider our past understanding of race as little more than a social construct. As such, ethnic and cultural identity are more relevant to the purpose of this paper. Not that race is irrelevant, rather, it is less useful in exploring the issues to follow. While race may be absolutely necessary in discussing criminal justice disparities in the U.S., in many parts of the world, such as Africa, the citizens' race may be homogeneous, but their cultures and identities may vary widely, with numerous tribes, communities and belief systems at the heart of disparities and unfairness in the legal system.[6]

While the 10% or so of the population described as LGBTQ+ cannot rightfully be considered as a single culture or community, as the qualities of each letter have their own individual characteristics, and share few similarities (Hutt, 2018), for the purposes of this paper, these people, representing a wide variety of unusual sexual preferences and gender identities, will be regarded together as one group. It is also relevant to note that, while gender is not considered a cultural marker *per se*, in many of the world's societies, women and girls are often treated differently under the law, although globally, as of 2017, the male population only outnumbered females by about 6 million, out of a total of approximately 7.5 billion humans on the planet.[7] **[see Figure 1 below]**

Rank	Sex	Estimated World Population
1	Male	3,776,294,273
2	Female	3,710,295,643

Source: worldatlas.com/articles/are-there-more-men-or-women-in-the-world.html

Before proceeding, it is also important to note Li & Karakowsky's admonition in a 2001 *Journal of Psychology* study, wherein they argue that "consideration of cultural differences is critical when applying observation techniques in cross-cultural research… [and the] potential for discrepancies in observer judgment making… affirm[s] the importance of (accounting for) cultural influences in research..."[8] In other words, unless the observer is a member of the culture under scrutiny, their findings will be prone to discrepancies, misunderstandings, and faulty judgements. That said, the observations here are limited by the author's own cultural milieu, and as such, correlations and reflections made herein are also duly limited insofar as understanding, relevance and import are concerned.

Multiculturalism and Diversity as Related to the Criminal Justice Systems

Across the planet, most contemporary societies reflect some level of cultural diversity, meaning that, although there may be a primary culture, with majority standing, the population of each sovereign state consists of numerous different cultures, as determined by ethnicities, religions, customs, tribal identities, or other such features. This has all come about through a range of causes, depending upon the part of the world under consideration, from migration and displacement, to colonization, war and genocide.[9]

Growing awareness and concern about how minority cultures are treated under the various legal systems enforced throughout the almost 200 nations across the planet has been sparked by activists in the human rights domain, as well as theorists in the fields of criminal justice and sociology.[10]

A 2016 study focusing on numerous problems in how to administer justice in multicultural societies examined a series of vendetta killings in the Netherlands involving an extended family of ethnic Kurds. The Dutch had not seen these kinds of related revenge homicides in over a hundred years, but such an incident in the mid 90's unleashed a wave of deaths that seemed to have no end in sight. In considering all the facts in a 2002 case, the fifth connected with this series of vendetta killings, the Dutch court allowed the plausibility that such a vendetta situation may generate so much fear that self-defense is justified, and they let the perpetrator go free. The study's authors noted that "Criminal law might serve any number of functions (retribution, crime prevention, rehabilitation), but settling disputes or dealing with vendettas is not one of them."[11]

These same authors pointed to the vast numbers of international immigrants who have steadily populated all of Europe since the close of WWII, and they observed that while there may be firm procedures in criminal justice, in the investigations, prosecutions and the punishment stage, it is quite commonplace across the EU to take a defendant's ethnic and cultural background into account.[12]

Women, Girls and LGBTQ+

Spurred in part by the widespread practices of female genital mutilation (FGM), particularly in Africa and South Asia, forced marriages, often of pre-pubescent girls, and domestic violence, in 2011 the Council of Europe introduced the Convention on Preventing and Combating Violence Against Women and Domestic Violence, also known as the Istanbul Convention.[13]

The criminal justice systems in the countries where such barbaric practices take place, as well as and other questionable behaviors targeting females, often uphold and support the concepts of culture and traditions, and those charged with such crimes often invoke what's come to be known as the "cultural defense" as a justification.[14]

The Istanbul Convention supports a system of international regulations that challenge the allowance of religion, tradition or culture to justify such violations of basic human rights. To date, only 45 nations have signed and ratified the Istanbul Convention, including all members of the European Union (EU). The U.S., Canada and Mexico, among many others, have yet to even participate in discussions with the sponsoring organization, the Council of Europe.[15] Among this convention's important assertions are the following:

- The state has a responsibility to prevent all forms of violence against women, protect those who experience it and prosecute perpetrators.
- The state must promote equality between women and men and prevent violence against women by encouraging mutual respect or non-violent conflict resolution and questioning gender stereotypes – including through teaching materials in schools.
- The state must ensure a coordinated approach among all relevant agencies, civil society organisations (*sic*) and other stakeholders to support those who experience violence and protect them from further violence.
- The state must investigate allegations of violence and prosecute perpetrators.[16]

There are about a dozen more bullet points such as these, in addition to provisions addressing prevention, professional training, raising awareness about these issues, and much more, a total of 81 individual articles, each with numerous details listed.[17]

To date, there has be no such international convention addressing the human rights abuses suffered by those who identify as LGBTQ+, which includes gay men, lesbians, trans gender, intersex, non-binary, and other uncommon sexual behaviors, identities, and physiological features.[18]

While homosexuality and transgender were once considered mental health disorders, neither the American Psychiatric Association, nor the World Health Organization have classified these as such for over a decade. However, although gay and trans rights have made significant advances in recent years, there are 73 nations, primarily in the Mid-East, Africa and Asia, where any kind of homosexual activity is illegal, with some only criminalizing sex between men, but an increasing number of countries enacting laws to include bisexuals and lesbian women, and in at least eight nations, any kind of homosexuality is punishable by death.[19] **[see Figure 2 above]**

By contrast, in the U.S. same-sex couples have the legal right to marry in all 50 states, however 31 states allow employers to not hire or to fire workers for being trans. Currently, trans Americans do not enjoy many of the hard won civil rights that gay men and lesbian woman have been garnering. In addition, hate crimes again trans people, especially those belonging to minority races, have been increasing, especially homicides.[20]

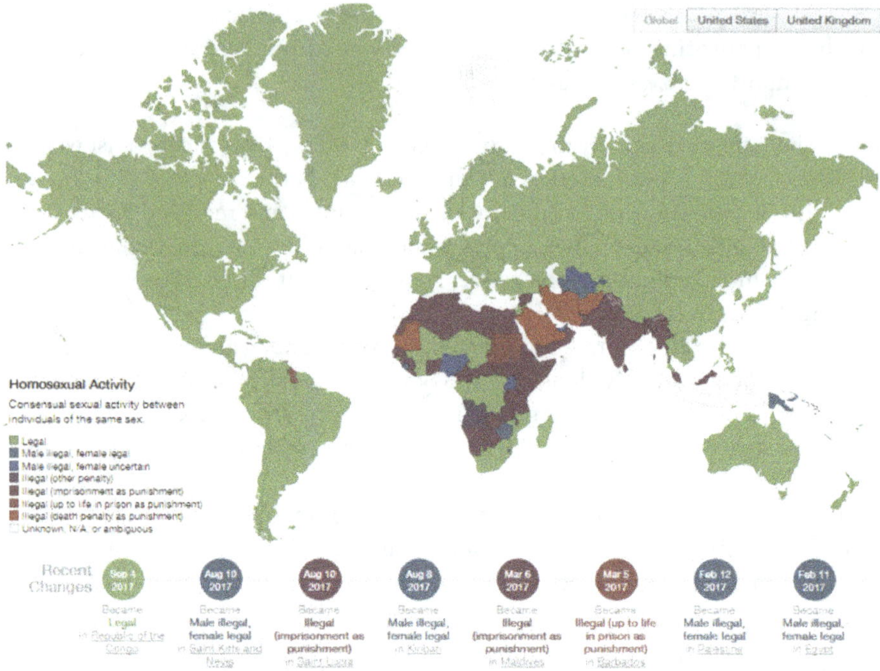

Source: https://www.weforum.org/agenda/2018/06/lgbti-rights-around-the-world-in-2018/

Conclusion

Oxford researcher Clara Rigoni, in her extensive 2018 exploration of cultural defenses and diversity in the world's various legal systems, observes that the ever expanding multiethnicity of global society might affect the consistency and effectiveness of our various criminal justice systems. However, she describes some innovative new ways of approaching some of the legal situations that have been made more complex due to cultural conflicts, through the advances and expanded use of alternative dispute resolution procedures and restorative justice, which provide some further options for taking culture into account in dispute resolution. Rigoni believes that these alternatives may point to one way that allows for a certain degree of access to justice for minority groups.[21] This also points to one possible adaptation that criminal justice systems across the planet could employ to bring more equality as the population continues to diversify.

ENDNOTES

1. UN, n.d.
2. Rosenburg, 2019.
3. Rosenburg, 2019.
4. TAMU, 2019.
5. Vocabulary.com, n.d.
6. Carter, 1995.
7. Miaschci, 2017.
8. Li & Karakowsky, 2001.
9. Rigoni, 2018.
10. Rigoni, 2018.
11. Bovenkerk & Yesilgoz, 2016.
12. Bovenkerk & Yesilgoz, 2016.
13. Rigoni, 2018.
14. Rigoni, 2018.
15. COE, 2019.
16. COE, 2019.
17. COE, 2019.
18. The Center, 2019.
19. Hutt, 2018.
20. ACLU, 2019.
21. Rigoni, 2018.

REFERENCES

ACLU, (2019), LGBT rights. Retrieved from https://www.aclu.org/issues/lgbt-rights

Bovenkerk, F.,Yesligoz, Y., 2016, Crime, Ethnicity and the Multicultural Administration of Justice, retreived from https://dspace.library.uu.nl/bitstream/handle/1874/11946/Bovenkerk_04_Crime,+Ethnicity+and+the+Multicultural+Administration+of+Justice.doc?sequence=2

Carter, R. T. (1995). The influence of race and racial identity in psychotherapy: Toward a racially inclusive model. Retrieved from https://psychology.iresearchnet.com/counseling-psychology/identity-development/racial-identity/

Council of Europe, (2019), What is the Istanbul Convention? Who is it for? Why is it important? Retrieved from https://ec.europa.eu/justice/saynostopvaw/downloads/materials/pdf/istanbul-convention-leaflet-online.pdf

Hutt, R., (2018), This is the state of LGBTI rights around the world in 2018. Retrieved from https://www.weforum.org/agenda/2018/06/lgbti-rights-around-the-world-in-2018/

Li, J., Karakowsky, L., (2001), Do we see eye-to-eye? Implications of cultural differences for cross-cultural management research and practice. Retrieved from https://www.tandfonline.com/doi/abs/10.1080/00223980109603715

Miaschi, J., (2017), Are there more men or women in the world? Retrieved from worldatlas.com/articles/are-there-more-men-or-women-in-the-world.html.

Rigoni, C., (2018), Crime, diversity, culture, and cultural defense. Retrieved from https://oxfordre.com/criminology/view/10.1093/acrefore/9780190264079.001.0001/acrefore-9780190264079-e-409

Rosenburg, M., (2019), The difference between a country, state, and nation. Retrieved from https://www.thoughtco.com/country-state-and-nation-1433559

Texas A&M University, [TAMU] (n.d.), Culture. Retrieved from http://people.tamu.edu/~i-choudhury/culture.html

The Center, (2019) What is LGBT?, Retrieved from https://gaycenter.org/about/lgbtq/

UN, (n.d.) Member states. Retrieved from https://www.un.org/en/member-states/

Vocabulary.com, (n.d.), Ethnicity. Retrieved from https://www.vocabulary.com/dictionary/ethnicity

6

Asian Americans and the Criminal Justice System

bgrocker/Shutterstock.com

Introduction

This chapter will present some aspects of how Asian Americans are reflected in the criminal justice system, as related to their history, gang and other criminal activity, representation in law enforcement, victimization, arrest and incarceration trends, along with other relevant issues.

Defining Asian Americans

According to the Pew Research Center, people from Asian countries are currently the fastest growing group of immigrants in the U.S., growing just over 72 percent between 2000 and 2015, from about 12 million to over 20 million. By comparison, Hispanic immigrants increased by roughly 60 percent during the same period.[1]

Over 20 countries comprise the region where Asian Americans originated, with China and India representing the largest group. As of 2015, East Asians accounted for less than 40 percent of immigrants from that part of the world.[2] While Vietnamese and Cambodians provided many of Asia's emigres following the wars in those countries, and more recently, large numbers have been arriving here from Bhutan, Nepal and Myanmar.[3]

Asian American History in the Criminal Justice System

Arguably, among the most relevant issues regarding the history of Asian residents and the American criminal Justice system, would be the Chinese Exclusion Act of the Nineteenth Century and the internment of Japanese Americans during WWII.

During the middle 1800's, there was a significant increase in the number of Chinese coming to America, drawn at first by the Gold Rush, and then by the growing opportunities for steady work as America expanded into the western territories. However, their willingness to work for the lowest wages led to great resentment toward the Chinese from the native workforce.

In addition, the striking cultural differences helped to feed falsehoods and vicious stereotypes about the Chinese, and by mid-century, many Americans were clamoring for immigration restrictions. California, where most of the Chinese landed, led the way with a series of laws from 1850-1870 restricting business, housing and travel access for Chinese people.

Due a superseding US treaty with China, there were no federal restrictions on immigration at this time,[4] however, in 1882, the Chinese Exclusion Act was passed by Congress and signed by President Chester Arthur, enacting a ten year freeze on Chinese labor immigration. After the act expired, a series of additional federal restrictions on Chinese immigration was in effect until after WWII.[5]

Reacting to Japan's attack on Pearl Harbor in 1941, Executive Order 9066 was signed by President Franklin Roosevelt, sending all residents of Japanese descent to internment in isolated camps, set up in three western states. Almost 120,000 people, the vast majority being American citizens, were confined in these camps from 1942 to 1946. Released following the war, many of the former prisoners were never able to rebuild the lives they knew before, and for some time, many Americans held those of Japanese descent in very low regard.[6]

In 1988, President Reagan signed the Civil Liberties Act, which offered a formal apology and compensation of $20,000 to each of approximately 100,000 survivors from the camps.[7]

As for other historical connections to the criminal justice system, Asian Americans are the least studied racial group for criminal justice research due to their low rates of criminal activity, so there is not much authoritative extant work covering this subject.[8]

Criminal Activity and Gang Involvement

While there is not a universal consensus on what the term "**gang activity**" means, research shows that Asian American gang activity has been an increasing presence in the criminal justice system for well over a decade, disproportionately represented, considering their relatively small population. While Chinese gangs have been tracked since the late 1920's, and have been a staple of crime dramas, the current surge is being led by gangs of South Asians, notably Cambodians, Laotians and Vietnamese. It should be noted that gang activity in general across all ethnicities, dramatically began to rise beginning in the 2010's.[9]

As for all other criminal activity associated with the Asian American population, see **Figure 1** and **Figure 2** below.

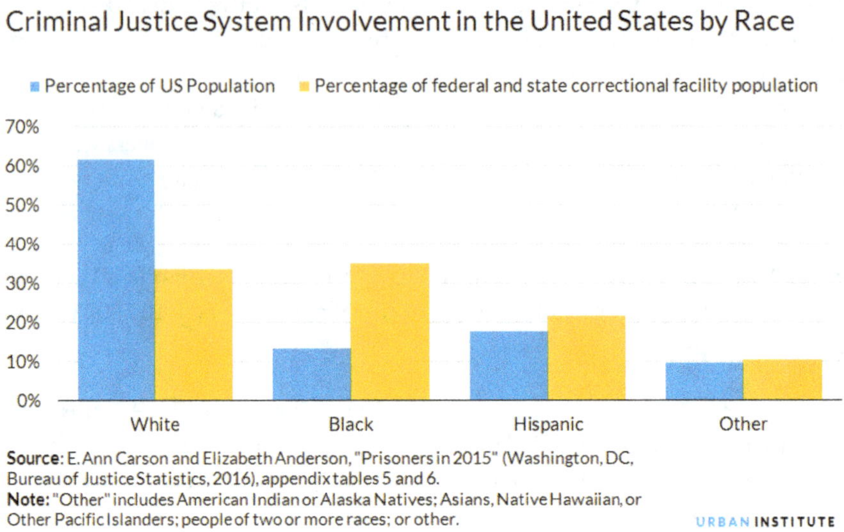

Figure 1

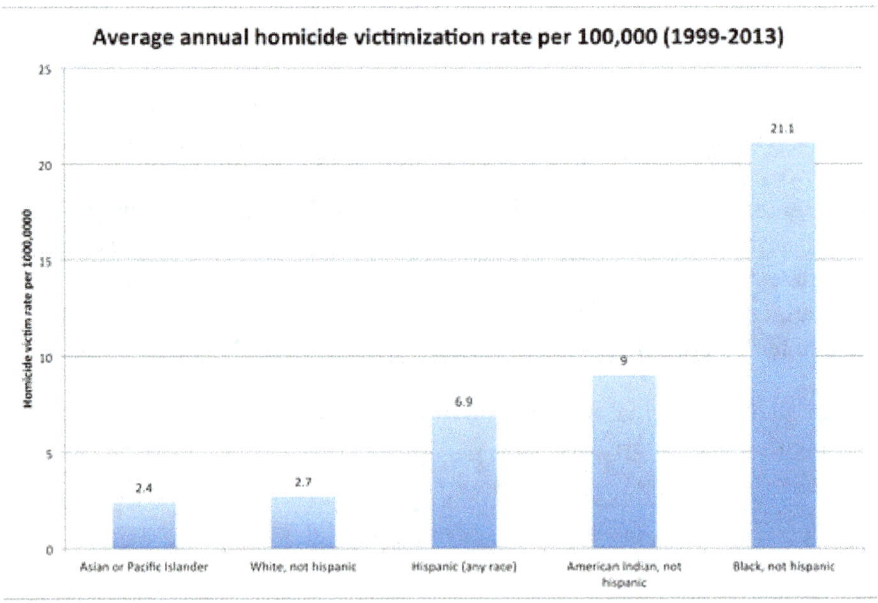

Figure 2
Source: https://randomcriticalanalysis.com/2015/11/16/racial-differences-in-homicide-rates-are-poorly-explained-by-economics/

Representation in Law Enforcement

Police officials across America are concerned that, while the number of Asian immigrants is expanding in U.S. cities, law enforcement agencies are having problems recruiting enough Asian-American officers in proportion to the communities they serve. Currently, only three percent of police officers identify themselves as Asian /Pacific Islander, whereas the last census places this population at 17.6 percent and this number has continue growing since then.[10]

ENDNOTES

1. Lopez, et al., 2019.
2. US Census Bureau, 2015.
3. Lopez, et al., 2019.
4. U.S. Dept. of State. n.d.
5. National Archives. n.d.
6. History.com., 2009.
7. NPR., 2013.
8. Sou, 2016.
9. Sou, 2016.
10. VOA., 2012.

REFERENCES

History.com Editors, (2009), Japanese internment camps. Retrieved from https://www.history.com/topics/world-war-ii/japanese-american-relocation

López, G., Ruiz, N.G., Patten, E., (2107), Key facts about Asian Americans, a diverse and growing population. Retrieved from https://www.pewresearch.org/fact-tank/2017/09/08/key-facts-about-asian-americans/

National Archives and Records Administration, (n.d.) Chinese Exclusion Act (1882). Retrieved from https://www.ourdocuments.gov/doc.php?flash=false&doc=47

NPR, (2013), From wrong to right: A U.S. apology for Japanese internment (transcript). Retrieved from https://www.npr.org/sections/codeswitch/2013/08/09/210138278/japanese-internment-redress

Sou, L., (2016), Asian gangs in the United States: A meta-synthesis. Retrieved from https://search-proquest-com.proxy.cecybrary.com/pq1academic/docview/1803939459/abstract?source=fedsrch&accountid=26967

U.S. Census Bureau, (2015), Retrieved from https://www.census.gov/programs-surveys/acs/news/data-releases/2015/release.html

U.S. Department of State, Office of the Historian, (n.d.), Chinese immigration and the Chinese Exclusion Acts. Retrieved from https://history.state.gov/milestones/1866-1898/chinese-immigration

VOA, 2012, US police departments face challenges recruiting asian-americans. Retrieved from https://www.voanews.com/archive/us-police-departments-face-challenges-recruiting-asian-americans

7

The Three Eras of Policing

Introduction

chippix/Shutterstock.com

This chapter will discuss what are commonly referred to as three eras of policing: The Political, the Reform, and the Community, providing a detailed summary of each, along with some of the impact that each era has had, or currently has, on policing practices and the criminal justice system.

Origins of The Three Eras of Policing

The three eras of policing are generally referred to as the Political Era, The Reform or Professional Era, and the Community Era. Some authors have suggested we have already moved into a fourth era, to be discussed later.[1]

Noted social scientist, James Q. Wilson, who taught at both UCLA and Harvard, is credited as a pioneer in his characterization of policing 'types,' which was introduced in the groundbreaking 1968 book, Varieties of Police Behavior.[2] Wilson defined certain performance styles of individual officers [**see Figure 1** below] and created the conceptual framework for the eras of American policing.[3]

James Q. Wilson

Legalistic Style: The emphasis is on violations of law and the use of threats or actual arrest to solve disputes in the community.

Watchman Style: The emphasis is on informal means of resolving disputes and problems in a community. Keeping the peace is the concern, and arrest is used only as a last resort to resolve any kind of disturbance of the peace.

Service Style: The emphasis is on helping in the community, as opposed to enforcing the law. Referrals and diversion to community treatment agencies are more common than arrest and formal court action.

Figure 1
Source: Policing: Roles, Styles, and Functions https://slideplayer.com/slide/9933795/

To this day, over a half century since publication, Wilson's book is a standard reference for defining and understanding police behavior. He was also one of the first to assert that the political culture in each jurisdiction contributes significant influence in the dissimilarities among various law enforcement agency practices.[4] His observations were foundational to the three eras concept.

In a 1988 Department of Justice report, Debating the Evolution of American Policing, a compilation of observations from numerous authorities in law enforcement and criminal justice, the editor notes that dividing policing into these three eras does not mean that there are distinct boundaries between each one, nor that there was ever a consistent, universal style of policing throughout the land. The eras primarily represent trends and tendencies.[5]

The Political Era

The Political Era covers the initial development of police agencies in municipalities across the U.S., beginning around the 1840s through the 1920s. In this era, officers of the law generally worked for the local politicians. They were not civil servants, but employees, hired, fired and overseen by elected officials. A police officer was expected to answer to and follow the direction of the police captain and the ward boss, who represented the smallest subdivisions of a municipality. Rookies were usually sent out with no training, experience or guidance, and being a cop provided low job security due to regular political turnover.[6]

In addition, driven as they were by politics, most police departments were inefficient and disorganized, frequently corrupt, doing little more than minding the political interests of elected officials, often as dangerous as the criminals they were supposed to be stopping. By the 1880s, urban reformers were pushing for laws to restrict the police from treating immigrants without regard to differing ethnic values. In addition, rampant corruption led to widespread clamoring for more control over the police.[7]

The Reform Era

The beginning of the Reform Era, also known as the Professional Era, is often associated with the Wickersham Commission, created by President Hoover in 1929, largely as a response to the soaring crime rate sparked by a decade of prohibition. Two of the commission's main recommendations were to separate police officers from the corrupting influence of politics, and to reduce the widespread prevalence of police brutality.[8] A nationwide civil service system was created, ending political control and manipulation in police staffing. Police departments ceased doing the bidding of politicians, and came to be known more as professionals, whose purpose was law enforcement.[9]

The Reform Era, which lasted into the 1970s, is noted for the introduction of specialized police training and dedicated academies, new management concepts and organizational structures, as well an increasing reliance on science and technology-- such as radio patrol cars, which dramatically changed police-community interactions--and forensic sciences, which vastly expanded investigative capabilities.[10]

The Community Era

During the late 1970s, legal scholars, particularly Law Professor Herman Goldstein, advocated that police needed to address the underlying dynamics contributing to crime, while Criminal Justice Professor Robert Trojanowicz added some structure to Goldstein's problem-oriented policing ideas, and called it "community policing," which featured an explicit police-citizen partnership toward solving those problems.[11]

Most of the earliest experiments in civilian-run review boards, police-citizen liaison groups, and other community-police partnerships were attempted in the late 1970s and 80s, and most of these trials were short-lived. However, the seeds were planted. Over time, numerous communities were able to demonstrate different kinds of collaborative programs that worked.

Community Policing received a significant boost with the 2015 publication of The President's Task Force on 21st Century Policing, which details many different scenarios that could be employed by localities large and small, designed to help reduce crime by improving the level of communication, trust, respect and cooperation between citizens and the law enforcement personnel who serve them.[12]

There is no one specific philosophy of community policing, nor a precise definition, and its practice may vary from one police department to the next. However, the foundational elements are essentially the same, members of the community want to feel that their police department is responsive, attentive, respectful and receptive to their feedback. In addition, the police must work in collaboration with the community in some way, to reduce crime and promote a shared sense of lawfulness.[13]

[See Chapters 4 and 17]

Conclusion

These loose timelines help to track the development of policing styles since pre-Civil War times to the present, although there are no clear cut boundaries separating the eras. It is fair to say that prevailing trends and common practices are reflected within those time frames. Policing in America started out with the

Political Era, corrupt and chaotic, and that was addressed, to a large extent, in the Reform Era, beginning with the Wickersham Commission, after which policing became a legitimate profession, with training, structure and ever more efficiency through a growing technological arsenal. With the 21st Century, as the trend heads more toward Community Policing, law enforcement agencies will want to practice Wilson's 2nd and especially 3rd styles of policing.

The literature is pushing against the confines of just three eras, with substantial claims that Homeland Security has become the fourth era, after being created as a response to the terror attack on 9-11, especially given its elaborate and far reaching role in American law enforcement and the number of agencies involved. In the President's Task Force report cited above, numerous Community Policing recommendations are integrated with preventing terrorism. Other authors assert that it is now the Information Era, given the role of computers and communication technology in today's policing, making this also a fair claim for defining a fourth era.

ENDNOTES

1. Oliver, 2007.
2. Bauer, 2012.
3. Zhaoa, et al, 2006.
4. Zhaoa, et al, 2006.
5. US DOJ, 1988.
6. Community Policing, n.d.
7. Hooper, 2014.
8. Harvard Law School Library, n..d.
9. Hooper, 2014.
10. Community Policing, n.d.
11. Hooper, 2014.
12. The President's Task Force..., 2015.
13. Community Police, n.d.

REFERENCES

Bauer, P., (2012), Janes Quinn Wilson. Retrieved from https://www.britannica.com/biography/James-Q-Wilson

Community Policing (n.d.), History of policing. Retrieved from http://www.communitypolicing.com/history-of-policing

Harvard Law School Library, n.d., United States Wickersham Commission records. Retrieved from https://hollisarchives.lib.harvard.edu/repositories/5/resources/6474

Hooper, M. K., (2014), Acknowledging existence of a fourth era of policing: The Information Era. Journal of Forensic Research and Crime Studies. Retrieved from http://citeseerx.ist.psu.edu/viewdoc/download?doi=10.1.1.687.7304&rep=rep1&type=pdf

Oliver, W.M., (2007), The fourth era of policing: Homeland security. Journal International Review of Law, Computers & Technology Volume 20, 2006 - Issue 1-2.

The President's Task Force on 21st Century Policing 2015 Final Report of the President's Task Force on 21st Century Policing. Retrieved from https://cops.usdoj.gov/pdf/taskforce/taskforce_finalreport.pdf

U.S. Department of Justice, (1988), Debating the evolution of American policing. Retrieved from https://www.ncjrs.gov/pdffiles1/nij/114214.pdf

Zhaoa, J. Heb, N., Lovrichc, N., (2006), The effect of local political culture on policing behaviors in the 1990s: A retest of Wilson's theory in more contemporary times. Journal of Criminal Justice. Retrieved from https://www.sciencedirect.com/science/article/pii/S0047235206000870

8

Ethical Issues in Managing Law Enforcement Agencies

New Africa/Shutterstock.com

Introduction

Being a leader of a Law Enforcement Agency (LEA), is a complicated, high pressure position, requiring wide-ranging capabilities to oversee a staff of personnel with different levels of competence, responsibilities and dispositions. The nature of the job is hard enough, having to deal with day to day matters involving literal life and death issues, various criminal activities, the protection of the public, political considerations, and funding issues, among other things, but that job becomes even more difficult when having to deal with some measure of misbehavior on the force, from that of a relatively petty nature, to fairly substantial corruption and illegal activities. Understanding the whys and wherefores of such behaviors, and the challenges they can cause, may also help in creating innovative strategies for LEA leaders to eliminate these misbehaviors and hold errant personnel accountable.

Standards of Ethics, Morality, and Legality in Law Enforcement Organizations

According to the Online Etymology Dictionary, the term *ethics* is derived from the ancient Greek, meaning the proper principles of a person or group. *Morals* is a more recent term, from the 1600s, describing human behavior as related to what is right and what is wrong. *Legality* originated from Roman times, and concerns issues that pertain to the law.[1] These three concepts are foundational to the practice of Criminal Justice, and essential to how we choose, as a society, to define criminal activity. Indeed, our Criminal Justice system cannot operate effectively without ethics, morals and legality.[2]

In 1957, the International Association of Chiefs of Police (IACP) established the Law Enforcement Code of Ethics (LECE), which has long since been accepted as the standard for criminal justice organizations across the U.S.[3] While there have been some minor revisions and fine-tuning since it was first introduced over a half century ago, within its six paragraphs, the LECE simply and eloquently defines the specifications for ethical and moral behavior by sworn police officers. It begins with a description of the basic job, being to serve the community, safeguard individuals, protect the innocent, and to respect the Constitutional rights of all. It goes on to detail the obligations for officers to keep their private lives exemplary and "unsullied," to live honestly, courageously, obey all laws, always be mindful of the welfare of others, and to never allow "personal feelings, prejudices, political beliefs, aspirations, animosities or friendships" to affect their professional decisions. The LECE also specifically prohibits taking part in any acts of corruption or bribery, and it requires a pledge to participate in any investigations of such activities. Finally, the officers swear to "take every reasonable opportunity to enhance and improve (their) level of knowledge and competence."[4]

The IACP also created an additional, shorter Law Enforcement Oath of Honor (**Appendix 1**), designed to be adaptable to any type of law enforcement agency from any nation. In this brief oath, officers swear that they will never betray their badge, their integrity, their character, or the public trust. They also assert their promise to behave with courage and accountability.[5]

In his authoritative book, *Introduction to Criminal Justice*, Kenneth J. Peak, former chair of the Department of Criminal Justice, University of Nevada, Reno, who also served a long and varied career in law enforcement, includes a chapter on police ethics, entitled "Ethical Essentials: Doing Right When No One Is Watching." It opens with a quote from an anonymous poet, which sums up not only how one develops a moral and ethical character, but also how one can wind up on the so-called 'slippery slope,' (to be addressed further in the next section).

> Watch your thoughts, for they become words.
> Watch your words, for they become actions.
> Watch your actions, for they become habits.
> Watch your habits, for they become character.
> Watch your character, for it becomes your destiny.

Peak offers some questions and situations designed to help determine ethical and moral behavior, as reflected through a variety of different actions, including whether or not one is using simple common sense; if the officer would feel comfortable if the public, the news media, or an admired person, such as minister or relative, found out what they had done; whether or not the actions caused pain for someone else; and finally, whether the behavior was worth jeopardizing their career.[6]

The staff of Northwestern University's graduate program of Law & Criminology offers some cogent observations about ethics in Criminal Justice, observing the importance of understanding the influence that ethical behavior will have upon how police engage with their communities, and conversely how the communities relate to them. When the citizens can see for themselves that their law enforcement officers are honest and ethical in dealing with them, the community in turn is far more likely to treat the police more openly and ethically.[7] Further illuminating this concept, the Wales' College of Policing website offers a page on Ethics, wherein the section on "Integrity and Transparency" expands upon Northwestern's ideas, reflecting that it goes well beyond just the public's perception of whether or not they feel that their local police are directly involved in corrupt behavior, but, perhaps even more importantly, the public's direct experiences with how police make everyday decisions, and how they treat individuals in the communities in which they serve, stating that, "If the public don't trust the police to be fair and act ethically and in their best interests, the evidence suggests they will be more likely to break the law and less inclined to help the police."[8]

Challenges That Law Enforcement Leaders May Face in Ensuring Correct Behavior and Accountability from Their Personnel

As with any organization, leaders in Law Enforcement Agencies (LEA) need to feel that they can rely upon the integrity and ethical behavior of their personnel. However, unlike most other organizations, the ramifications and repercussions of misbehavior among the ranks of LEA employees can have more serious, dire, and possibly even life-threatening consequences.

At its simplest, police corruption involves some form of attaining personal gain through the misuse of their authority. In the aforementioned book, *Introduction to Criminal Justice*, Peak notes that police corruption can be defined on a spectrum, from relatively inconsequential types of unethical behavior, such as expecting a local sandwich shop to provide free lunches once in a while, to major wrongdoing, like shakedowns, or illegally selling weapons. However minor it may start out, those first steps across the line into unethical activity, such as accepting small gifts, can all-too-easily lead to a 'slippery slope,' whereby officers begin to expect, and then demand gifts of a greater and greater value.[9]

In a 2016 NIJ funded study, conducted by researchers at Bowling Green State University, researchers identified 6,724 cases involving the arrests of 5,545 sworn officers across the nation between 2005 and 2011, with some 40% of the crimes being committed on duty. This mean that police officers are getting arrested around 1,000 times per year (Ferner, 2016).

The IACP's Law Enforcement Code of Conduct was mentioned earlier. One of the biggest challenges the LEA leaders face is also another unwritten, code, which has long persevered throughout many of America's LEA's, referred to by one writer, in a 1968 issue of the *Journal of Law and Criminology*, as the Informal Code of Police Deviancy. University of Texas Professor of Sociology and Anthropology, Ellwyn Stoddard, described eight practices of this code, including *mooching*- or expecting gratuities on the beat, such as free meals, drinks, small items, etc., accompanied by a sense of entitlement from feeling underpaid; *chiseling* – demanding discounts and freebies, whether related to the job or not; *favoritism* – using licenses and other official papers to gain undeserved immunity and privilege, even extending it to family members; *prejudice*- routinely treating minorities unfairly; *shopping*- essentially shoplifting small items when a store entrance is found to be unlocked on patrol; *extortion* – demands for money, goods or services in exchange for canceling a citation or arrest; *bribery* –receiving cash or gifts with the promise of preventing or derailing future prosecutions; *shakedown* – stealing expensive items during the investigation of a break in or burglary; and *perjury*- the expectation and demand that fellow officers will lie and provide alibis for co-workers who have been arrested for unlawful activity, also known as the Blue Code of Silence.[10]

In 2000, the National Institute of Justice (NIJ), the research, development and evaluation agency of the U.S. Department of Justice (DOJ), issued a report entitled "The Measurement of Police Integrity," an exploratory, qualitative study that sought to measure officers' attitudes towards various kinds of police misconduct. The method of inquiry asked officers from thirty different U.S. agencies to respond to eleven different examples of corrupt behavior. The researchers believed that if they presented hypothetical scenarios, rather than ones based on real, observed experiences, the respondents would be more likely to offer their true opinions on each situation, thereby providing more a more accurate representation of their authentic attitudes.[11]

The eleven imaginary cases in the study included such misbehaviors as a cop running his own, off-book, private security firm, while still on the force; officers routinely getting free meals, cigarettes, and other items of value from the merchants on their beat; pocketing valuables, such as watches and necklaces, from a crime scene; and choosing to not report a fellow officer who was found to be drunk behind the wheel at an accident, among other such scenarios. In their findings, the researchers determined that most police officers would not report a fellow officer who had committed what they believed to be relatively minor misconduct, such as running the private security business, accepting gifts, and causing accidents without injury. However, most cops said that they would report those who stole from a crime scene, accepted bribes to overlook criminal behavior, or who used excessive force on a non-violent suspect, such as a burglar. The researchers also found significant variations in what they termed the 'environment of integrity' among the thirty different agencies surveyed.[12]

This concept, the environment of integrity, will be explored further at some length in the next section. However, it bears more consideration here, as the creation and maintenance of such an atmosphere can only happen if the police personnel have a well-grounded understanding of the concept even before they are recruited into the LEA as rookies. Most states require some kind of ethics education at the academy level prior to an individual becoming a sworn officer, but there are considerable differences in the length, style and quality of preservice academy training, from as little as 3 months, to a half year or longer. Even then, the literature reveals that less than four hours of that training is devoted to ethics. In addition, over 80% of all police recruits only have a high school education, and no academy training at all. Beyond that, on the job, in-service ethics instruction is virtually non-existent in the 18,000+ LEAs in the U.S.[13]

These are just some of the major challenges that law enforcement leaders may face in expecting correct behavior and accountability from their rank and file police employees.

How Law Enforcement Leaders May Best Address Problems in Behavior and Accountability Among Their Personnel

The previously mentioned NIJ researchers, along with several other writers of related literature, noted that there has been very little in the way of systematic, quantitative research studying the phenomenon of police corruption, and the environment of integrity. The NIJ group offered two broadly different paradigms related to what they believed lead to LEAs of integrity. One is the Administrative/Individual Theory of Corruption, which postulates that misbehavior from the rank and file is seen as morally defective and will not be tolerated, therefore all such miscreant officers, and recruits who seem prone to and such behaviors, are presumed to be expunged from the LEA. The other paradigm is the Organizational/Occupational Culture Theory of Corruption, wherein the agency of integrity has managed to create a culture that tends to be highly resistant to corruption.[14] Both models must stem from the character of the leadership.

On-going, high quality ethics training for all LEA personnel is indispensable in order to establish and maintain an environment of integrity. Police personnel must be able to understand the concrete connections between written agency policies and actual conduct on the street through practical, hands-on training that underscore the rules and expectations of behavior (Wyatt-Nichol & Franks, 2009). These regularly scheduled ethics trainings should be job-specific instruction for all officer ranks and agency positions and should continue throughout each officer's career. The educational subject matter should incorporate specific decision-making models, explore the values involved, and include exercises in critical thinking.[15]

Funding for such on-going trainings are available through a variety of venues, such as the Police Grants Help bulletin, provided by Police One, arguably the most popular source of information for the U.S. Policing community on the internet. Police Grants Help claims to track billions of dollars available for LEA projects.[16] Another source of funding would be the Peace Officer Standards and Training (POST) program, which may vary from state to state. In Colorado, the state legislature funds the POST "for continuing education training of Colorado peace officers."[17]

In addition to ethics training, leadership by example would be another important piece in creating and maintaining an environment of integrity, as rank and file cops will take notice of the ethical conduct of their leaders and will tend to model their own behavior on that basis.[18] The leaders must also take the time and energy to educate themselves about some fundamental basics of human behavior, insofar as they relate to better promoting moral and ethical behavior among their personnel. This extends to an understanding of how they can motivate officers to inform on the unethical behavior of their peers.[19] It also involves routinely informing personnel of which kind of conduct is acceptable and which is unacceptable through a consistent, well-timed, and sensible system of reward and penalty. [20]

Another related area for leadership attention in addressing misbehavior and accountability on the force is to understand some of the known psychological factors, and mental dispositions, that have been known to erode a recruit's ethical resolve due to the nature of the job, particularly a traditional overemphasis on how dangerous it is to be an officer. Although one's well-being and security should be acknowledged, training could also represent the dangers more truthfully to avoid implanting new recruits with an unrealistic picture of how threatening this occupation actually is.[21]

One more idea that an LEA leader may want to consider in order to better address misbehavior and accountability among the department personnel is the establishment of a civilian review board, which is a community based group of local citizen representatives whose task it is to investigate complaints by members of the public pertaining to reports of police officer misconduct. Such a board may be conducted independently, or as part of a collaboration with the law enforcement agency. The literature is unclear about the overall effectiveness of the over 140 local such review board in the U.S., however, anecdotally, the presence of such a body seems to improve police community relations, and the public attitude toward having such oversight leads to a perception of less police corruption in their localities. Understandably, it has often been reported that members of the local force are opposed to such a board, but there are indicators that when officers know they may be held accountable by a civilian panel, it tends to deter the most egregious of police misbehaviors.[22]

[see Chapter 4]

Conclusion

Police officers hold a unique occupation in the community, having tremendous authority which they can use to help or hurt the civilians they serve. As detailed above, there is an abundance of ways in which a police officer can break the rules of morality, legality and good ethics, and numerous motivations for doing so. The LEA leader must address these challenges through recognizing and understanding the characteristics of corruption on the force, and countering such malfeasance with determination and resolve. One of the many responsibilities of the LEA leader is to reign in all such misbehaviors, without exception, while also establishing and maintaining an atmosphere of ethical conduct throughout the agency. Presented above are some suggestions for how that can happen. Intelligent, motivated and resourceful leaders can certainly add their own innovations to this list.

Appendix 1

LAW ENFORCEMENT OATH OF HONOR

"On my honor,
I will never betray my badge,
my integrity, my character,
or the public trust.

I will always have the courage
to hold myself and others
accountable for our actions.

I will always uphold the Constitution,
the community,
and the agency I serve,
so help me God."

Source: https://www.vachiefs.org/oath_of_honor

ENDNOTES

1. Online Etymology Dictionary, 2020.
2. Northwestern University, 2016.
3. Wyatt-Nichol & Franks, 2009.
4. International Association of Chiefs of Police [IACP], 2020.
5. Virginia Association of Chiefs of Police, 2020.
6. Peak, K.J., 2019.
7. Northwestern University, 2016.
8. College of Policing, 2020.
9. Peak, K.J., 2019.
10. Stoddard, 1968.
11. Klockars, et al, 2000.
12. Klockars, et al, 2000.
13. Wyatt-Nichol & Franks, 2009.
14. Klockars, et al, 2000.
15. Gaffigan & McDonald, 1997.
16. Police Grants Help, 2020.
17. Colorado.gov, 2020.
18. Wyatt-Nichol & Franks, 2009.
19. Kargin, 2011.
20. Fitch, 2011.
21. Blumberg, et al, 2018.
22. Goldsmith & Lewis, 2000.

REFERENCES

Blumberg, D.M., Papazoglou, K., Creighton, S., (2018), Bruised badges: The moral risks of police work and a call for officer wellness. Retrieved from https://www.omicsonline.org/open-access/bruised-badges-the-moral-risks-of-police-work-and-a-call-for-officer-wellness-1522-4821-1000394-101995.html

College of Policing, (2020), Integrity and transparency.. Retrieved from https://www.college.police.uk/What-we-do/Ethics/integrity-and-transparency/Pages/Integrity-and-Transparency.aspx

Colorado.gov, (2020), Colorado Peace Officer Standards and Training. Retrieved from https://www.colorado.gov/pacific/post

Ferner, M., (2016), Here's how often cops are arrested for breaking the laws they're paid to uphold. Retrieved from https://www.huffpost.com/entry/cops-arrested_n_576c2e13e4b0cedfa4b9470f

Fitch, B.D., (2011), Rethinking ethics in law enforcement. Retrieved from https://leb.fbi.gov/articles/focus/focus-on-ethics-rethinking-ethics-in-law-enforcement

Gaffigan, S.J., McDonald, P.P., (1997), Police integrity: Public service with honor. Retrieved from https://www.ncjrs.gov/pdffiles/163811.pdf

Goldsmith, A., Lewis, C., (2000), Civilian oversight of policing: Governance, democracy and human rights. Retrieved from https://www.bloomsburyprofessional.com/uk/civilian-oversight-of-policing-9781841130309/

International Association of Chiefs of Police, (2020), Law enforcement code of ethics. Retrieved from https://www.theiacp.org/resources/law-enforcement-code-of-ethics

International Association of Chiefs of Police, (2020), The oath of honor. Retrieved from https://www.theiacp.org/resources/the-oath-of-honor

Kargin, V. (2011), Peer reporting of unethical police behavior. Retrieved from https://www.ncjrs.gov/App/Publications/abstract.aspx?ID=260386

Klockars,C.B., Ivkovich, S.J., Harver, W.E., Haberfeld, M.R., (2000), The measurement of police integrity. Retrieved from https://www.ncjrs.gov/pdffiles1/nij/181465.pdf

Northwestern University Graduate Program Staff, (2016), 3 ways ethics influence criminal justice. Retrieved from https://www.northeastern.edu/graduate/blog/3-ways-ethics-influence-criminal-justice/

Online Etymology Dictionary, 2020, Ethics. Retrieved from https://www.etymonline.com/word/ethic

Peak, K.J., (2019), Introduction to Criminal Justice. Retrieved from https://www.sagepub.com/sites/default/files/upm-binaries/59357_Chapter_4.pdf

Police Grants Help, (2020), Your resource for police department & law enforcement grant assistance. Retrieved from https://www.policegrantshelp.com/

Stoddard, E.R., (1968), Informal code of police deviancy: A group approach to blue-coat crime. Retrieved from https://scholarlycommons.law.northwestern.edu/jclc/vol59/iss2/5/

Virginia Association of Chiefs of Police & Foundation, (2020), Law enforcement oath of honor. Retrieved from https://www.vachiefs.org/oath_of_honor

Wyatt-Nichol, H., Franks, G. (2009), Ethics training in law enforcement agencies. Retrieved from https://www.researchgate.net/publication/240051009_Ethics_Training_in_Law_Enforcement_Agencies

9

The Status of Women in American Policing

John Roman Images/Shutterstock.com

As of 2021, 60.3 percent of full-time civilian employees in US law enforcement agencies were women, but only 13.3 percent of full-time law enforcement officers were women, whereas 86.7 percent of officers were male, and less than 3 percent of police chiefs were female.[1] Louisiana boasts the highest proportion of women officers, at just over 22%, while West Virginia reports the lowest at 3.3%.[2] Statistics like these are cautionary warnings for leaders in law enforcement, especially for those who understand that local police should mirror the populations in which they serve.[3] Margo Frasier, Police Monitor for Austin, TX, observed, "We make better decisions when those who are making the decisions for the community look like the community."[4]

Deborah Friedl, a 30-year veteran with the Lowell, MA, Police Department, and the first woman to serve as their deputy superintendent, expressed frustration that women have gotten almost no attention in policing. Dep. Superintendent Friedl, who is also vice president of the International Association of Women Police Officers, describes how discouraged she feels at this late stage of her career, "There's no energy about doing anything to recruit women or show any effort to do your best to recruit women."[5]

Although decades of research have established the benefits of increasing women's representation in policing,[6] according to a report from the National Center for Women and Policing (NCWP), the numbers of women in law enforcement are kept artificially low purposefully through widespread discriminatory hiring practices.[7] The NCWP has been promoting plentiful and convincing research which clearly indicates that the surest pathway toward lowering the rates of violence against women -- including sexual assault, rape, and murder -- is to recruit more female officers.[8] Those are not the only benefits to be gained by increasing the number of women in the nation's police agencies.

As reported by the NCWP, over twenty years of extensive research strongly indicates that women police officers generally employ a quality of policing based on far less physical force than traditionally used by their male counterparts, and they also rely much more on communication skills, which are known to be more effective in defusing potentially violent situations. Reports also indicate that female officers are far less likely to perpetuate incidents of police brutality. Assistant Police Chief Crystal Young-Haskins, of the Little Rock, AR, Police Department explains, "We hear the public when they criticize us about excessive force. There's research out there that says that women are better de-escalators. They don't resort to force first, they communicate first, and then uses of force become a last resort."[9]

Female officers also tend to be considerably more effective when responding to situations involving violence against women, which comprise the largest category of calls to police agencies across the U.S.[10] This is further underscored by crime-victimization data indicating that as female police presence increases in any given area, reports of crimes against women, particularly domestic violence, come in at significantly higher rates,[11] which means that those victims have a better chance of putting a stop to the abuse as compared to situations that go unreported.

Austin Police Monitor Margo Frasier's observation that those who are making the decisions for a community should look like that community, strongly suggests that police leadership across the US should seriously overhaul recruitment and retention practices insofar as women are concerned. For one example, specifications for strength testing are almost universally based upon male physical characteristics, where upper body strength is an advantage. In states like New Jersey, female recruits and sworn officers fail these tests at three times the rate of males. However, if such testing was readjusted to account for lower body strength, female officers would not be at such an unfair disadvantage.[12]

The old-fashioned, authoritarian style of top-down management is typical in many, if not most, of America's 18,000 police departments, along with the quasi-military tradition of 'don't question orders,' which generally trickles down to reinforce authoritarian policing styles, where law enforcement takes charge of any given engagement without much room for civilian input. This management style is not amenable to the gentler, more humanistic approach generally exhibited by female officers, who have a proven track record of being able to diffuse tense situations with a more cooperative, communicative approach.[13]

One of the most forward-looking proposals to show up recently is the **30 by 30 Initiative**, a national movement promoting the notion of having 30% of America's sworn police officers be women by the year 2030. This initiative is comprised of a coalition of police leaders, researchers, and professional organizations who have joined together to advance the representation and experiences of women in all ranks of policing across the United States, built upon decades of research that shows the unique benefits women officers bring to policing agencies, such as those already discussed here, and more. **30 by 30** has garnered active support from over 300 police agencies nationwide and is also promoted by the US Dept of Justice.[14,15]

Just a few examples have been presented here that point to some of the positive long-term effects likely to result from recruiting and hiring more women as law enforcement officers, in addition to some of the changes required to improve female representation and effectiveness in America's police departments. Heading into the future, it is the leadership of this nation's police agencies who will need to take on the necessary commitment to advance the training and hiring of capable women, vital assets, who have been overlooked and underused for far too long.

ENDNOTES

1. Duffin, 2022.
2. Ford, 2019.
3. Ramsay 2021.
4. Wedell, 2017.
5. National Center for Women & Policing, 2020.
6. Policing Project at NYU School of Law, 2021.
7. National Center for Women & Policing, 2020.
8. Asquith 2018.
9. Goldsmith, 2022.
10. Spillar, 2015.
11. Asquith 2018.
12. Ford, 2019.
13. Ford, 2019.
14. Policing Project at NYU School of Law, (2021)
15. Goldsmith, 2022.

REFERENCES

Asquith, C., (2018), Why aren't U.S. police departments recruiting more women? Retrieved from https://www.theatlantic.com/politics/archive/2016/08/police-departments-women-officers/497963/

Duffin, E., (2022), Gender distribution of full-time U.S. law enforcement employees 2021. Retrieved from https://www.statista.com/statistics/195324/gender-distribution-of-full-time-law-enforcement-employees-in-the-us

Ford, A., (2019), Can American police close the gender gap? Retrieved from https://thecrimereport.org/2019/08/06/can-american-police-close-the-gender-gap/

Goldsmith, M., (2022), More police departments are hiring women, here's why. Retrieved from https://www.thv11.com/article/news/local/police-departments-more-women-recruits/91-ef6d1985-e10e-43bc-9f6d-b1c0cdf17575

National Center for Women & Policing, (2020), Changing the face of policing. Retrieved from http://womenandpolicing.com/

Policing Project at NYU School of Law, (2021), 30 X 30: Advancing Women in Policing: 30% Women Recruits by 2030. Retrieved from https://30x30initiative.org/

Ramsay, A., (2021), Diversity in policing: An educational assessment. Retrieved from https://www.blueline.ca/diversity-in-policing-an-educational-assessment

Spillar, K., (2015), How more female police officers would help stop police brutality. Retrieved from https://www.washingtonpost.com/posteverything/wp/2015/07/02/how-more-female-police-officers-would-help-stop-police-brutality/

Wedell, A., (2017), Women in law enforcement. Retrieved from https://www.n-r-c.com/gender-balance-law-enforcement/

10

How Race, Social Class, or Common Stereotypes May Influence Officer Decision Making

rblfmr/Shutterstock.com

Decision Fatigue

There are numerous factors that require attention when considering how police officers determine what course of action to take in any given situation that may come up when they are on patrol, not the least of which are the complex dynamics involved in making decisions. To make an effective decision, one must consider the circumstances, deliberate the options, then choose the action that seems likely to result in the most favorable outcomes.

Former Chief Investigator for the Illinois State's Attorney Office, Laura King, who also holds a PhD in Psychology, offered an extensive examination of 'decision fatigue,' in *Police Chief* magazine, which runs evidence-based articles by practitioners in law enforcement and related fields. Noting that decision fatigue is a well-known effect resulting from the limited amount of power available to the human mind for decision-making on a daily basis, for most people, including cops, it is easier to make stress-free, appropriate decisions earlier in the day, whereas, toward the end of a long shift, there is a measurable lack of energy and higher stress levels that can impact even the simplest decisions. Statistics have shown that there is a significant drop off in late-in-shift arrests that hold up, regardless of race or ethnicity of the individuals arrested.

Dr. King asserts that it is vitally important for supervisory law enforcement personnel to understand what is involved in this common phenomenon and address it directly in trainings and in reviewing performance issues. She points out that while law enforcement has long recognized and acknowledged what happens to the brain when it is exposed to the usual pressures related to police operations, it is not just high-stress situations that may negatively impact an officer's judgement, but also ordinary daily routines and behaviors, even diet, can influence their brains in ways that may compromise the ability to perform at their best, which includes decision making.[1]

Best Practices for Officer Decision Making

While biological cycles are clearly involved in following the best course of action, so are decision making skills, which can, and should, be learned, as opposed to winging it from situation to situation, or simply responding 'by the book' to whatever is encountered on patrol.

Noting that past research on police behavior has focused on actions taken by officers following contact with a citizen, with a conspicuous void in attention paid to the process by which police officers form suspicion about a potential suspect before a formal intervention, such as a stop, was made, a 2004 Department of Justice study examined the police officers' decision making process prior to initial contact being made, and the thinking involved in the formation of suspicion. The conclusion is that more attention must be given to what goes on in the officer's mind well before they confront a citizen.[2]

Lt. Dan Marcou, highly decorated, thirty year law enforcement veteran, and police trainer from Wisconsin, believes that effective decision making must be cultivated from young recruits on, and he offers 12 steps to being a more decisive cop in a 2017 article in *Police One*, one of the primary internet sites covering what's current in American policing. Here are his headlines. I recommend clicking on the link in the references for his insightful descriptions of each.

1. **Look for opportunities to critically think**
   (critical thinking is the basis for ALL sound decisions, especially in criminal justice.)
2. **Understand authority**
3. **Train to be prepared**
4. **Give positive and timely critique**
5. **Experience counts**
6. **Proper tools enable officers to take action**
7. **Words of encouragement**
8. **Instill confidence**
9. **Maintain training**
10. **Desire**
11. **Courage**
12. **The ability to decide**[3]

Race & Ethnicity Bias in Officer Decision Making

There is a startling statement in the introduction of a major report by the National Academies of Sciences, Engineering, and Medicine (NAS) on the effects of proactive policing on communities and crime:

> **"The high rates at which non-Whites are stopped, questioned, cited, arrested, or injured by the police present some of the most salient criminal justice policy phenomena in the United States."**[4]

The report notes that researchers have been aware for decades of the stop and arrest rates in relation to demographic groups, and the various racial disparities throughout the criminal justice process, and within offender and victim statistics. In addition, history reveals long standing explicit animus and racial bias in a significant number of jurisdictions against non-Whites.[5]

Clearly, this is not simply a relic of the past, in fact, since 2006 the FBI has been warning that local law enforcement agencies across the country are being infiltrated by white nationalists, which is not just happening by coincidence. This is an intentional and coordinated program being promoted through the white supremacist culture. To date there have been personnel scandals involving ultra-racist cops in over a hundred police departments in 40 states, and the number of such recruits does not seem to be abating.[6]

ENDNOTES

1. King, 2019.
2. US DOJ, 2004.
3. Marcou, 2017.
4. NAS, 2018.
5. NAS, 2018.
6. Johnson, 2019.

REFERENCES

Johnson, V. B., (2019), KKK in the PD: White supremacist police and what to do about it. Retrieved from https://law.lclark.edu/live/files/28080-lcb231article2johnsonpdf

King, L., (2019) Decision Fatigue and Why It Should Be Understood by Law Enforcement Leadership: Can Science Provide Insight into How Officers Make Decisions? Retrieved from https://www.policechiefmagazine.org/decision-fatigue/

Marcou, D., (2017), 12 steps to being a more decisive cop. Retrieved from https://www.policeone.com/police-training/articles/459318006-12-steps-to-being-a-more-decisive-cop/

National Academies of Sciences, Engineering, and Medicine. 2018. Proactive Policing: Effects on Crime and Communities. Washington, DC: The National Academies Press. https://doi.org/10.17226/24928.

U.S. Department of Justice, (2004), Police Officers' Decision Making and Discretion: Forming Suspicion and Making a Stop. Retrieved from https://www.ncjrs.gov/pdffiles1/nij/grants/213004.pdf 2004

11

The Influences of Organizational Culture in Law Enforcement Decision Making

arindambanerjee/Shutterstock.com

As detailed in a joint report by the Harvard Kennedy School and the National Institute of Justice (NIJ), today's American police forces must deal with a wide variety of issues that were generally not on the radar of law enforcement during previous eras of policing. These include responding to threats from foreign and domestic terrorists, active shooters in public facilities, more complicated immigration issues, a runaway opioid use epidemic, and crimes related to internet use, among other present dangers. Because of these, along with all other additional contemporary pressures, police organizations must adjust and evolve if they hope to remain effective in these times.[1]

However, there are also long entrenched forces at play that tend to thwart adaptability to changing circumstances on the part of many police agencies at all levels, local, state and federal. Perhaps the most prominent of these forces are long ingrained organizational cultures. According to one study, sworn police officers have long thought of themselves, and behaved as though, they were separate from the general public, which helps to foment doubt and wariness of civilians. In addition, effective inter-agency collaborations between the law enforcement, correctional workers, and public service personnel are often strained, or even adversarial. For instance, police consider public service workers as outsiders, who cannot comprehend "real" police work or the importance of their day to day tasks. This 'us vs. them' attitude negatively influences police trust of those they consider to be outsiders, and certainly has an impact on decision-making by officers.[2]

A Walden University study points to the impactful nature of police decision-making on the public's perceptions and attitudes toward law enforcement, noting that street-level encounters with civilians often have immediate as well as long lasting effects. Poor judgments and bad decision-making by officer's lead to an erosion of trust, acceptance, respect and validity from the community, and can cause more violent confrontations between police and citizens. The same study finds that the culture of the local police force influences the officers' outlook, opinions and approaches toward the public, and once these attitudes are entrenched, there is a heightened reluctance toward any acceptance of new training programs or implementation of different procedures for dealing with the public.[3]

One of the most important influences in recent years affecting new directions in officer training and decision-making is the advent of Community Policing, formally introduced in the mid-1990's by the U.S. Department of Justice through their Community Oriented Policing Services, or COPS, program. According to the information released when COPS first began, the DOJ stated that "rather than simply responding to crimes once they have been committed, community policing concentrates on preventing both crime and the atmosphere of fear it creates." Further, the DOJ asserted that through earning the community's trust and treating individuals in the community as contributors, with a vested interest in their own safety, as opposed to 'outsiders' who have no place in combating law breaking, police personnel can improve their own understanding and better address community needs, especially as related to the factors that contribute to crime.[4]

The 2015 President's Task Force on 21st Century Policing emphasized the need for law enforcement personnel to learn how to work more closely with the communities in which they serve, through a variety of innovative collaborations with local merchant and civic organizations, as well as increased direct interactivity with the civilian population. Such changes are seen as vital in addressing the contemporary crime problems mentioned above, such as domestic terrorism, immigration issues, cybercrime and so on.[5]

In localities where Community Policing is successfully being implemented, studies have shown that front line officers are increasingly accepting that the most significant impact on decision-making is not only their on-the-job experiences, but that community policing can create more positive experiences. Such findings can enhance positive changes, and more acceptable decision-making by police personnel, when officers and community members collaborate as joint stakeholders in developing trainings for more positive social relationships and cultural awareness between officers and citizens.[6]

[see Chapters 4 & 17]

ENDNOTES

1. Batts, et al, 2012.
2. Bodor, et al, 2004.
3. Anthony, 2018.
4. US DOJ, 2017.
5. US DOJ, 2015.
6. Anthony, 2018.

REFERENCES

Anthony, L.D., (2018), Police culture and decision-making, Retrieved from https://scholarworks.waldenu.edu/cgi/viewcontent.cgi?article=6881&context=dissertations

Batts, A.W., Smoot, S.M., Scrivner, E., (2012), Police Leadership Challenges in a Changing World. Retrieved from https://www.ncjrs.gov/pdffiles1/nij/238338.pdf

Bodor, T., Thompson, F., & Demircivi, F., (2004), Criminal justice culture in the United States: A context for understanding aspects of organizational change. Retrieved from https://www.ctg.albany.edu/media/pubs/pdfs/hpa_2004_criminal.pdf

US Department of Justice, (2017) Community Policing [COPS]. Retrieved from https://www.justice.gov/jmd/file/822291/download

US Department of Justice, (2015), Final Report of The President's Task Force on 21st Century Policing. Retrieved from https://cops.usdoj.gov/pdf/taskforce/taskforce_finalreport.pdf

12

False Convictions in Death Penalty Cases

Introduction

This chapter concerns issues raised in an article by Gross, *et al*, entitled Rate of False Conviction of Criminal Defendants Who are Sentenced to Death, which examines U.S. death row statistics from approximately three decades. Some of the most relevant aspects of the authors' findings related to improper guilty verdicts in capital cases will be discussed, along with problematic implications insofar as the criminal justice system is concerned. Possible measures that may help prevent such wrongful convictions will also be considered here.

Photo Spirit/Shutterstock.com

Relevant Findings from Gross, et al, in Their False Conviction Death Penalty Study

A thought provoking study published in the Proceedings of the National Academy of Sciences in 2014, entitled Rate of False Conviction of Criminal Defendants Who are Sentenced to Death, examined US death penalty records from 1973 through 2004. The starting date of 1973 was chosen as it is considered as the beginning of the nation's so-called modern death penalty era, after the U.S. Supreme Court invalidated all death sentencing laws prior to that year. According to the Bureau of Justice Statistics (BJS) of the Department of Justice, 7,482 defendants were sentenced to death in the United States during the period covered by the study, with 1,320 having been executed.[1]

While the authors acknowledged that there are no infallible methods available to determine the correctness of a criminal trial verdict, and that the rate of erroneous convictions of innocent defendants is commonly considered to be unknowable, they based their research on the known exoneration rate for defendants who had been mistakenly convicted in death penalty cases, deciding that this would offer a reasonable proxy for the rate of false convictions. Starting with that exoneration figure, their study utilized a combination of several statistical evaluations, employing a medically based model known as survival analysis, along with the Kaplan–Meier methods of estimation, and other quantitative procedures, after which the authors determined that as many as 4.1 percent of those facing capital punishment were erroneously convicted, which they also assert is most probably an undercount, and that, quoting from the report, "there are more innocent death row defendants who have not been identified and exonerated than guilty ones who have been exonerated in error." In either case, these findings cast significant doubts upon the integrity of the arrest, conviction and appeals procedures in such cases, along with other potential shortcomings and drawbacks in our criminal justice system.[2]

Among the ramifications that the authors discussed in their study was the likelihood that those exonerations resulted in large part from the intense scrutiny that often surrounds death penalty cases, especially as the execution date draws nearer, backed up by what they refer to as a wealth of anecdotal evidence suggesting that judiciary and political leaders or more likely to weigh the importance of considering the possibilities of innocence at that time, therefore increasing deliberations on whether to reverse a conviction or to commute a death sentence to life imprisonment. The authors also note that once a death sentence is commuted to life, the intensity of that scrutiny fades, and exoneration of innocent convicts becomes even far less probable. They also emphasized that they were unable to draw any conclusive corollaries linking their findings to the number false convictions for other kinds of crime, as murder cases, particularly involving capital punishment, are treated quite differently than other criminal cases.[3]

Implications for the Criminal Justice System Regarding Wrongful Convictions

Prior to the publication of the Gross study, a commonly held and oft-expressed belief among criminal justice professionals was that the number of wrongful convictions was negligible. Justice Antonin Scalia wrote in a 2007 U.S. Supreme Court opinion that America's criminal convictions have an error rate of .027 percent.[4] The authors of the Gross study flatly assert that Scalia's claim is ridiculous, as the conviction information he employed was based upon dubious numbers and questionable math, and the justice's conclusion could not have possibly been ascertained from such unreliable data. Although fewer such assertions have been forthcoming in the wake of the Gross study, with additional literature generally supporting their findings, the authors note that there is no shortage of legal professionals who still confidently state that the number of false convictions is insignificant.[5]

Clearly it is problematic to hold such a fallacious view, as this can easily lead to a false sense of complacency, perhaps obscuring what may otherwise be obvious mistakes in judiciary proceedings. In a 2013 American University report funded by the National Institute of Justice (NIJ) several common factors were identified that helped lead to wrongful convictions of innocent defendants. These included younger defendants being more likely to be wrongly convicted, a prevailing punitive culture in the state where the trial takes place, a defendant's past criminal history, a weak prosecution case which too often withholds pertinent information, misidentification of witnesses, misstatements by witnesses, misinterpreted forensic data, and other related issues. The study also presented several recommendations to reduce and prevent flawed convictions in the future, which included the importance of addressing police misconduct.[6]

A separate study the following year, Policing and Wrongful Convictions, conducted jointly by the NIJ and the Harvard Kennedy School Program in Criminal Justice Policy and Management, addressed the role of law enforcement in the problem of false guilty verdicts, beginning with the arresting and investigating officers' cognitive biases coming into play early in the process. The study also emphasized the importance of employing best practices throughout the investigation, including ascertaining all eyewitness identification, avoiding false confessions, verifying informant testimony and preserving evidence. The study also stressed the need for police to maintain an openness to learning from error and interpreting mistakes as representative of system-wide weaknesses.[7]

Conclusion

As discussed above, in the course of arresting and trying a defendant for a capital murder charge, there are a number of elements that can derail justice and lead to a wrongful conviction. According to the Innocence Project, a non-profit legal organization committed to exonerating the falsely convicted, in addition to those factors already mentioned, mistaken identification is one of the primary factors leading to wrongful convictions, along with problems involving cross-racial identifications, as witnesses too often fail to properly distinguish features of people from another race. Such subtleties may determine guilt or innocence in the mind of a jury. They also cite prosecutorial misconduct as another problem, such as failure to share relevant exculpatory evidence, and similar misconduct by investigators. In addition, people who can't afford to hire an attorney must rely upon public defenders, who are usually buried under a mountain of caseloads and chronically underfunded, making them less effective, and resulting in lower-income people failing to receive the robust defense they deserve.[8]

Clearly, as discussed, there are some serious lapses in the criminal justice system that can lead to wrongful convictions, which are particularly egregious when an individual's life is at stake. Even 4.1 unjustifiable deaths out of 100 executions are too many.

ENDNOTES

1. Gross, et al, 2014.
2. Gross, et al, 2014.
3. Gross, et al, 2014.
4. Campbell, 2008.
5. Gross, et al, 2014.
6. NIJ, 2013.
7. Batts, et al, 2014.
8. Grawert, 2018.

REFERENCES

Batts, A.W., deLone, M., Stephens, D.W., (2014), Policing and wrongful convictions. Retrieved from https://www.ncjrs.gov/pdffiles1/nij/246328.pdf 2014

Campbell, W.A., (2008), Exoneration inflation: Justice Scalia's concurrence in Kansas v. Marsh. Journal of the Institute for the Advancement of Criminal Justice. Retrieved from https://www.cjlf.org/files/CampbellExonerationInflation2008.pdf

Grawert, A., (2018), Wrongful convictions: Why they happen, and why they can be so hard to fix. Retrieved from https://www.brennancenter.org/blog/wrongful-convictions

Gross, S. R., O'Brien, B., Hu, C., & Kennedy, E. H. (2014). Rate of false conviction of criminal defendants who are sentenced to death. Proceedings of the National Academy of Sciences. Retrieved from https://www.pnas.org/content/111/20/7230

National Institute of Justice, (2013), Predicting and preventing wrongful convictions. Retrieved from https://www.nij.gov/topics/justice-system/wrongful-convictions/Pages/predicting-preventing.aspx

13

The US and the International Criminal Court (ICC)

DCStockPhotography/Shutterstock.com

Introduction

The United States government has generally opposed an International Criminal Court (ICC) that could assert jurisdiction over and prosecute U.S. military or political leaders according to an established global standard of justice. This chapter will present policy programs that allow criminal justice agency leaders from other nations to collaborate with the U.S. in a formal global effort to address terrorism and transnational crime, and will also address a number of other relevant concerns, ranging from how such partnerships are managed, to the benefits and costs to the U.S., as well as some of the elements required to make these cooperative efforts effective.

About the ICC and U.S. Opposition to It

The ICC was established in 2002 as a permanent, authoritative judicial body designed to prosecute crimes of genocide, crimes against humanity and war crimes. While 137 countries signed the 1998 Rome Statute, which formed the criteria and purpose for creating the court, currently, there are 123 participating countries.[1] Some powerful nations -- Russia, China and India, along with the United States -- have declined to join the ICC, concerned about several issues, such as weak procedural safeguards, criminal charges being politically driven, and potential infringements on national autonomy.[2] To date, the ICC has indicted 44 individuals, issued arrest warrants for 36 persons, and summonses to eight others. There are a half dozen accused confined in detention, with ongoing criminal proceedings currently being pursued against another 22. The ICC is also monitoring 11 situations world-wide that are within their purview under provisions of the Rome Statute.[3]

To one degree or another, every U.S. Administration since the court was formed has continued to oppose joining, citing, among other concerns, the ICC's extensive authority with no accountability to the U.N. Security Council, potential violations of national sovereignty by declaring jurisdiction over citizens and military teams of non-party states and, as mentioned, the absence of safeguards against political manipulation.[4] The U.S. helped to derail at least one ICC investigation into accusations of atrocities committed by American soldiers in Afghanistan, though a campaign of blocking ICC personnel travel, and other aggressive maneuvers, which many member-states saw as overbearing.[5]

In a 2007 debate at Cornell University concerning the pros and cons of the ICC, Jeremy Rabkin, Cornell professor of government, argued against U.S. involvement in the court, stating that such a global law enforcing entity would fail for numerous reasons. In one example, Rabkin asserted that this international court system may provide the illusion of a remedy without actually fixing anything. Citing the atrocities occurring at that time in Uganda as one example, he pointed out that it was more important for nations to join together in order to stop the fighting, rather than only focusing on prosecuting those committing the crimes.

Rabkin also noted that the ICC has no actual enforcement body of its own, and if any outside country decided to send its own troops to quell inter-tribal warfare, or genocide, it would then risk having its own army being prosecuted by the ICC, as he stated, "There is no mechanism within the ICC to facilitate such a tradeoff between peace and justice."[6]

In addition, after a very slow start in accomplishing any of its stated goals through the early years, more recently the court has experienced a number of disconcerting setbacks, from ponderously slow investigations, to poorly mounted prosecutions, to negative interference from non-party states, including the U.S., and other impediments to effectually operating the ICC.[7]

Positive Perspectives, Influences and ICC Adjacent Activities

While acknowledging numerous difficulties and shortfalls, as compared to the high aspirations when the ICC was first created, some authors on the subject also recognize affirmative and constructive aspects of the ICC that provide insights to certain ancillary positive effects, outside the courtroom, regardless of the tribunal's many limitations. For instance, in the wake of a recent Colombian civil war, the quiet presence of ICC investigators is believed to have helped reign in some of the post war tumult, and influenced a sense of accountability going forward. The U.N. created a special entity, the International, Impartial and Independent Mechanism (IIIM), collecting investigative files which may be accessed for future prosecution, and to cover crimes that the ICC has chosen not to address. Even just the existence of the court has been seen by some to have inspired vigorous independent prosecutions of cases declined by the ICC, such as a group of European nations, including France and Germany, after the ICC decided not to address war crimes in the Syrian conflict committed by al-Assad.[8]

The intentions and purposes of the ICC are not confined to the Rome Statute, to the member states, or to a courthouse in The Hague, but also reflect the efforts of a multitude of national authorities, regional human rights organizations, and civilized societies, all of which appear to be steadily reinforcing a global objective to address crimes against humanity.[9]

The U.S. has often responded with humanitarian aid, through governmental agencies and Non-Governmental Organizations (NGOs), in situations of ethnic conflict, where crimes against humanity are commonplace. However, as noted in a 2009 Council on Foreign Relations report, directly responding to those situations with military force or 'police action' is constrained by international legal practices and any significant show of force requires extensive international consultation, especially in the United Nations Security Council, before such troop movements can be authorized.[10]

With the specific purview of the ICC being to prosecute individuals for the international crimes of genocide, crimes against humanity, war crimes, and crimes of aggression, such as human trafficking and slavery,[11] along with constraints on direct intervention by armed forces, America's law enforcement efforts aimed at stopping terrorism, and other transnational criminal enterprises must turn to entities outside the ICC for collaborative investigative operations involving international criminals.

INTERPOL, Information Sharing with ICC, and Other Collaborative Efforts

Even thought the U.S. is not a party to the ICC, its relationship with the court is not always obstructionist or adversarial. There are numerous instances when American officials from the federal government, including the Departments of Justice, State and various armed forces, have sat in as observers, advisors, and information sharing operatives in ICC investigations, such as during a 2010 conference addressing war crimes and crimes against humanity in Uganda.[12]

In addition, the U.S. is a fully participating member in INTERPOL, also known as The International Criminal Police Organization, along, with 195 other countries. While not a corporeal police force, per se, since its creation in 1923, INTERPOL has established a highly efficient system of information sharing, providing investigative support and communications between law enforcement authorities throughout INTERPOL's member countries, as well as availing access to their extensive databases, resources, and services. While there are no INTERPOL enforcement personnel as such, the agency does issue Red Notices, akin to arrest warrants, alerting members with identifying information on the criminal, the charges and their suspected whereabouts. Member states are not required to act on these notices, and American authorities have occasionally rejected making arrests from Red Notices due to 4th Amendment concerns, however, the U.S. will usually at least notify appropriate authorities to "be on the look-out" for the fugitives in question, and to advise if they have a possible location. The U.S. also gets to issue its own Red Notices.[13]

Through the Federal Bureau of Investigation's (FBI) legal attaché, or Legat program, the Bureau is able to conduct its work combating international terrorism, organized crime, cybercrime, and other far ranging criminal matters across the globe. The mission of the Legat programs is to establish and maintain liaisons with the primary law enforcement and security service agencies in designated foreign countries, aimed to prevent terrorist attacks against citizens and American interests. The Legat activities are carried out in accordance with applicable U.S. executive orders, statutes, treaties, Attorney General Guidelines, FBI policies, and interagency agreements. Currently, FBI special agents and support professionals are working in about 80 overseas operations, tracking terrorists, intelligence breeches, and criminal threats across an international landscape, while also participating in global and regional crime-fighting enterprises, in addition to INTERPOL, along with transnational strategies where FBI and DEA agents worldwide are embedded with foreign agencies to combat drug trafficking.[14]

The National Institute of Justice (NIJ) is the research, development and evaluation agency of the U.S. Department of Justice, essentially contributing to the fight against crime through science.[15] The work of the NIJ has been steadily expanding in its international reach, establishing partnerships and procedures with other countries, gathering and exchanging expertise between forensic researchers, and cooperating in the development of new information. Technological development has proven to be a very productive field for international law enforcement collaborations, and the NIJ's International Center chief, stated that in cases where the crimes may originate overseas, America's law enforcement agencies are able to gather crucial insights from research that is not just focused on U.S. interests.[16]

International Law Enforcement Collaboration Costs and Benefits to the U.S.

In financial terms, U.S. spending on internationally collaborative law enforcement operations is relatively modest. For instance, in 2017, INTERPOL's total operating revenue was 124.3 million Euros, or about 137 million dollars, of which the U.S. provided the equivalent of 10.4 million Euros in statutory membership fees in addition to 9 million or so for special projects, and in-kind value for providing FBI and other U.S. agency staff involvement.[17]

The FBI's Legat programs cost approximately 40 million dollars out of a total budget of just under 9 billion,[18] while the NIJ's annual spending is about 48 million dollars, out of a total Department of Justice budget of some 25 billion.[19]

As has been suggested previously, there have been tangible benefits for America in its involvement with international law collaborations. INTERPOL has immeasurably improved international relationships and efficacy for law enforcement since it formed in the 1920s. Cooperative efforts have proven so positive and fruitful that even police personnel from countries who have no diplomatic relations frequently work together through the aegis of INTERPOL, to solve crimes and capture criminals.[20] A 2011 Center for Global Collective Action Working Paper reported that each dollar of counterterrorism spending by the U.S. with INTERPOL returns around $200 of worth, and the agency was rated highly for its efforts to organize counterterrorism strategies by its member nations that have led to arrests of terrorists and weakening their ability to continue operations.[21]

NIJ's International Center has provided funding for investigative partnerships with foreign nations whose citizens conduct criminal activities in the U.S., such as cooperation with El Salvador investigators, concerning the MS-13 gang, and information from Burma, home of drug smuggling operations, and even China, where smugglers were illegally arranging for people to enter the U.S. NIJ has been expanding its International Center to ensure that all of its research portfolios can be available for the U.S. criminal justice research community to learn from and share with other countries.[22]

These are just some of the material benefits to the U.S. by continuing to support such programs of international law enforcement cooperation.

Conclusion

The ICC, while initially created out of sense of shared purposes and a need for global cooperation, insofar as addressing crimes against humanity are concerned, has had difficulty living up to its promise, steadily weakening in effectiveness and support since its inception.

The limits of its purview and potential threats to national sovereignty, among other issues, have kept the U.S. from joining. However, this does not mean that Americans cannot join with other nations in meaningful collaborations to effectively combat terrorism and transnational crimes, especially those that may not be covered by the Rome Statute. The three primary examples described above, INTERPOL, FBI Legat, and NIJ, are just a few of many such efforts currently operating around the globe.

ENDNOTES

1. CNN, 2019.
2. Arora, 2007.
3. ICC, 2019.
4. Groves & Shaefer, 2009.
5. Goldston, 2019.
6. Arora, 2007.
7. Goldston, 2019.
8. Goldston, 2019.
9. Goldston, 2019.
10. Council on Foreign Relations, 2009.
11. Council on Foreign Relations, 2009.
12. US Dept. of State, 2010.
13. INTERPOL, n.d.
14. FBI, n.d.
15. NIJ [National Institute of Justice], n.d.
16. Bulman, 2008.
17. Bromund, 2019.
18. FBI, 2020.
19. US Department of Justice, 2019.
20. Roufa, 2019.
21. Sandler, et al, 2011.
22. Bulman, 2008.

REFERENCES

Arora, K, (2007), Two scholars debate whether U.S. should join International Criminal Court. Retrieved from http://news.cornell.edu/stories/2007/03/scholars-debate-us-policy-toward-international-criminal-court

Bromund, T., (2019), How large is the U.S. budgetary contribution to INTERPOL? Retrieved from https://www.heritage.org/global-politics/commentary/how-large-the-us-budgetary-contribution-interpol

Bulman, P., (2008), 'Internationalizing' criminal justice research. Retrieved from https://nij.ojp.gov/topics/articles/internationalizing-criminal-justice-research

CNN Editorial Research, (2019), International Criminal Court fast facts. Retrieved from https://www.cnn.com/2016/07/18/world/international-criminal-court-fast-facts/index.html

Council on Foreign Relations[CFR], (2009), Intervention to stop genocide and mass atrocities. Retrieved from https://www.cfr.org/report/intervention-stop-genocide-and-mass-atrocities

Department of Justice, (2018), FY 2018 budget request at a glance. Retrieved from https://www.justice.gov/jmd/page/file/968216/download

Federal Bureau of Investigation, (2020), FY 2020 budget request at a glance. Retrieved from https://www.justice.gov/jmd/page/file/1142426/download

Federal Bureau of Investigation, (n.d.) International operations. Retrieved from https://www.fbi.gov/about/leadership-and-structure/international-operations

Goldston, J. A., (2019), Don't give up on the ICC. Retrieved from https://foreignpolicy.com/2019/08/08/dont-give-up-on-the-icc-hague-war-crimes/

Groves, S., Schaefer, B., (2009), The U.S. should not join the International Criminal Court. Retrieved from https://www.heritage.org/report/the-us-should-not-join-the-international-criminal-court

ICC, (2019), Situations under investigation. Retrieved from https://www.icc-cpi.int/pages/situation.aspx

INTERPOL, (n.d.),How we work. Retrieved from https://www.interpol.int/en

Roufa, T., (2019), INTERPOL: International policing. Retrieved from https://www.thebalancecareers.com/interpol-international-policing-974516

Sandler, T., Arce, D.G., Enders, W., (2011), An evaluation of INTERPOL's cooperative-based counterterrorism linkages. Retrieved from http://research.create.usc.edu/published_papers/148

U.S. Department of Justice, (2019), INTERPOL Washington. Retrieved from https://www.justice.gov/interpol-washington/frequently-asked-questions

U.S. Department of State, (2010), U.S. engagement with the ICC and the outcome of the recently concluded review conference. Retrieved from https://2009-2017.state.gov/j/gcj/us_releases/remarks/2010/143178.htm

14

The US and Transnational Crime Concerns

PeopleImages.com - Yuri A/Shutterstock.com

Beginning in the 1980s, the US vigorously embarked on a program to disseminate America's criminal justice techniques and procedures, along with what were considered its "transnational crime priorities," to other nations.[1] Despite encountering significant resistance from many other countries, in large part due the disproportionate percentage of U.S. citizens being incarcerated, especially people of color, along with our very punitive, 'get tough on crime' measures,[2] thousands of American experts in the field of prosecution and police procedures travelled across the world intending to advance democracy and development, as well as to control crime by helping other cultures to reform their criminal justice systems using U.S. models. Through the intervention of organizations like the Justice Department's Office of Overseas Prosecutorial Development Assistance and Training (OPDAT), over two dozen countries adapted some of our criminal justice methodology, and the State Department's International Law Enforcement Academies trained thousands of police officers in a handful of countries as well.[3]

However, insofar as America's commitment to dealing with transnational organized crime is concerned, as described in Gastrow's 2013 report prepared for the Institute for Security Studies Policy, most U.S. voters, and the politicians they elect, focus far more on policing strategies that are short term, uncoordinated and confined to our own country, with almost no attention paid to transnational organized crime.[4] So it would seem that this nation's commitment to collaborating with other countries in such matters is unreliable and self-centered, in addition to being rooted in a draconian attitude toward the treatment of criminals, that is not shared or respected by most other civilized, developed countries.[5]

One example of transnational organized crime the U.S. seems to be more consistently committed to is the so-called War on Drugs, which began during the Nixon years in the 1970s, leading to collaborations with Mexico, Columbia and other sources of the massive illegal drug trade. While significant changes to these ongoing efforts took place during the Obama administration, with more of an emphasis on rehabilitation and mental health treatment, particularly for youthful addicts, there is still a prevailing trend toward working with other nations to try and prevent criminal importation of illicit substances, although the efforts remain somewhat inconsistent.[6] Add to this the proliferate legalization and decriminalization of cannabis across the U.S., and many of the formerly robust international cooperative efforts are considerably diminished, nor does it help that the worst addiction epidemic in American history is currently being driven by legal painkillers, which has in turn dramatically expanded the demand for easily hidden, and even more lethal substances, such as Fentanyl.

Focusing upon just these two areas that impact upon the U.S. involvement in combatting transnational organized crime -- excessive incarceration and the drug trade – perhaps we could benefit by importing forward thinking attitudes to address these problems from other countries, rather than assuming that 'American Exceptionalism' has all the answers. For instance, Portugal's daring choice to legalize all drugs in 2001 has dramatically transformed a dire social dilemma, and the results are demonstrably more positive than the way it was before.[7]

Portugal's substance abuse problem has improved substantially in a number of important areas, particularly in the radical reduction in HIV infections and drug-related deaths, while the extreme increase in drug use feared by many has not materialized. In addition, Portugal didn't just simply legalize problematic substances, but vastly expanded the allocation of funding to improve prevention, treatment, harm reduction and social reintegration.[8] In addition, Portugal is not the only country to have enacted such a reform, with some two dozen other nations having removed criminal penalties for the personal possession of some or all drugs.[9]

It is not likely that America will ever prevent people from using harmful substances, so perhaps we can take a cue from Portugal and revamp how we deal with this area of transnational organized crime.

Another area we could learn from other nations, and which may improve creating collaborative partnerships in combatting international criminals, is in overhauling our criminal justice and correctional systems. The U.S. attitude toward law breakers has long been one of punishment and retribution. We send our criminals to over-crowded, brutal penitentiaries, and maintain a recidivism rate as high as 65% in some states, quite unlike Sweden, which may boast the most enlightened correctional program on the planet.

In Sweden, which has far lower per capita incarceration and crime rates than the U.S., and revidism well below 40%, prison is about rehabilitation. "Our role is not to punish" observes Nils Öberg, director-general of Sweden's prison and probation service. "The punishment is the prison sentence: They have been deprived of their freedom." He also notes that some people need to be locked up, "but it has to be a goal to get them back out into society in better shape than they were when they came in." Correctional officers there are trained to help rehabilitate the prisoners, in a sense they serve as counselors more that simply enforcers. This reflects a more civilized approach to criminal justice, with more a humane perspective.[10]

This seems to be the goal of the recent advances in some of America's criminal justice reforms, such as the First Step Act, designed to release low level, non-violent offenders from incarceration,[11] which seems to be a positive advance in U.S. efforts to conform with the more humanitarian treatment of criminals in the rest of the civilized world, which may help to relieve some of the other nations' reticence to collaborate in combatting transnational organized crime.

ENDNOTES

1. McLeod, 2010.
2. Collier, 2014.
3. McLeod, 2010.
4. Gastrow's, 2013.
5. Aleem, 2015.
6. Valenzuela, 2013.
7. Transform, 2020.
8. Transform, 2020.
9. Rosmarin & Eastwood, 2013.
10. Aleem, 2015.
11. Clark & Ross, 2019.

REFERENCES

Aleem, Z., (2015), Sweden's remarkable prison system has done what the U.S. won't even consider. Retrieved from https://www.mic.com/articles/109138/sweden-has-done-for-its-prisoners-what-the-u-s-won-t

Clark, D., Ross, J., (2019), The First Step Act promised widespread reform. What has the criminal justice overhaul achieved so far? Retrieved from https://www.nbcnews.com/politics/politics-news/first-step-act-promised-widespread-reform-what-has-criminal-justice-n1079771

Collier, L. (2014). Incarceration nation. Monitor on Psychology, 45(9), 56. Retrieved from http://www.apa.org/monitor/2014/10/incarceration.aspx

Gastrow, P. (2013). Transnational organised crime: The stepchild of crime-combating priorities. Institute for Security Studies Policy Brief, 46, 1–4. Retrieved July 21, 2016, from https://www.issafrica.org/uploads/PolBrief46.pdf

McLeod, A. M. (2010). Exporting U.S. criminal justice. Yale Law & Policy Review, 29(1), 83-164. http://digitalcommons.law.yale.edu/cgi/viewcontent.cgi?article=1604&context=ylpr

Rosmarin, A. and Eastwood, N. (2013), A Quiet revolution: drug decriminalisation policies in practice across the globe. Retrieved from https://www.opensocietyfoundations.org/uploads/8c6213b8-9a9f-453a-9702-ff832f29afa5/release-quiet-revolution-drug-decriminalisation-policies-20120709.pdf

Transform, (2020), Drug decriminalisation in Portugal: Setting the record straight. Retrieved from https://transformdrugs.org/drug-decriminalisation-in-portugal-setting-the-record-straight/

Valenzuela, C.M., (2013), The "War on Drugs" and the "New Strategy": Identity constructions of the United States, U.S. Retrieved from https://www.sciencedirect.com/science/article/pii/S1870057816300257

15

Legislative Responses to Sex Crimes

Susan M Hall/Shutterstock.com

Introduction

This chapter seeks to illuminate some of the known intentions and agendas driving legislators when they write the laws and punishments related to sexually based offenses, and whether or not those policies are based upon empirical psychological and behavioral research, in addition to looking at the part that public opinion and commonly held misconceptions might play in developing these legal responses, as well as considering available data related to whether or not such laws work as the lawmakers intended them to.

This chapter also presents information, resources, and some successful models that may be valuable to concerned citizen activists, community mental health advocates, and professional treatment providers who may choose to get involved in the legislative process when laws related to sex offenses are being created or revised.

Introduction

Research indicates that most of the legal responses and punishments created to address the crimes of sexually based offenders are, more often than not, derived as much from commonly held misconceptions and groundless stereotypes, than from evidence-based practices (EBP) derived from psychological and behavioral science.[1] This is likely to impact whether such legal responses result in effectively protecting the public safety and whether they create the sought-after changes in the criminal behaviors of such offenders, as lawmakers intend.[2] Advocacy with legislators by informed, concerned citizen activists during the process of creating or revising sex offender policies may help to bring more EBP into relevant proposed legal remedies, thereby enhancing public safety, and encouraging positive behavioral and lifestyle changes in potential sex offenders as well.[3]

Sexually Based Offenses

Law enforcement and the criminal justice system have long grappled with how to handle the aberrance and perversity of sexually based offenses.[4] Sex crimes commonly evoke deep emotional responses quite unlike other sorts of violations, and significant research conducted about these phenomena to date points to troubling implications about the impact of stereotypes, popular myths, and proven misconceptions in the drafting of laws, penalties and treatment related to sex offenders.[5] This would include mandated psycho-therapeutic programs and other legal interventions required of those convicted of sex crimes, very often implemented without regard to the significant diversity in offender types, frequency and severity of their criminal behavior, the level of harm done to others, if any, or the psychological profile and personality characteristics of the individual offender.[6,7]

Sex Offender Management

The predominant style of sex offender management (SOM) currently in use by most federal and state correctional systems, is based upon a punishment/retribution paradigm, with prevention of any further such behavior being the foremost goal.[8] Some of the research has indicated that this strong hand approach might have some measurable effect on recidivism rates, the all-important standard for determining the effectiveness of the program,[9] however, that data represents a few relatively small studies, and a direct correlation has yet to be established. Conclusive research proving such a connection, and recidivism research related to these offenders may also be quite skewed, as the observers may well have anticipated a much higher number of repeat offenses, based upon popular misconceptions.[10] In short, we do not know whether all the time, effort, energy and money expended on SOM programs actually prevent reoffending any better than if there were no such programs at all.

Evidence-Based Alternatives

For convicted sex offenders, most SOM programs, at best, are a demanding mix of psycho-therapeutic interventions, behavioral mandates, and legal constraints, in a world full of considerable societal hatred.[11] Addressing some substantial shortfalls in the dominant correctional/punitive SOM approaches, also presented here are a few of the evidence-based standards that could illuminate new treatment perspectives and possibilities, with a different understanding about how behaviors may change, truly, and for life, through self-awareness based methodologies,[12] none of which are included in the roster of psychotherapeutic approaches associated with most of the America's SOM programs.

Legislative Responses to Sex Crimes

The state of Colorado represents a significant exception to the dominant trend as described above. Their Sex Offender Management Board (SOMB), an all-volunteer agency with oversight as to what happens with convicted sex offenders, was also expressly established to investigate and adopt the most promising EBP. The SOMB was created by the Colorado General Assembly in revising a prior statute, and some forward-thinking voices of reason were able to cut through the usual myths and misconceptions, and encourage the legislation to include the possibilities of innovations and more effective treatment methods, and to be open to EBP that may be unconventional or lesser known, even though legal constraints and coercive qualities may still be endemic to the SOM process,[13] but the Colorado legislature did open the door to new possibilities.

In describing the general trajectory of steps involved in the creation, approval and execution of various statutes and regulations relevant to sex offender management (SOM), herein we also track the extent to which commonly held misperceptions about 'those kinds' of criminals is intrinsic to the process, as well as how much of a role EBP in psychology and behavioral science plays in the policy makers' determinations, if at all.[14]

Although there may be some minor variations in details from state to state, concerned and determined citizens can get involved in the legislative process,[15] and attempt to promote an agenda of including more EBP in whatever SOM programs are being used in a given jurisdiction.

The Legislative Process

The inquiry presented here includes questions from three broad areas of relevance. The first involves a fairly detailed understanding of the legislative processes in the adoption of the various legal responses to sex crimes, in this case using the state of Colorado as an example.[16]

Like the federal legislature, Colorado's law-making body, the General Assembly, consists of two chambers, the state House and state Senate. A proposal, or bill, can be introduced by the legislators in either chamber of the General Assembly.

In the House, introduction of a bill takes place with a first reading by the House clerk, after which it is assigned to the appropriate committee by the Speaker of the House. In cases of SOM regulations that may be the Judiciary, or perhaps the Health and Human Services committee. From there, committee hearings will take place which will include public and expert testimony. This is when interested parties have an opportunity to influence the discussion. It is also a period during which amendments may be offered.

A passing vote from the committee sends the bill back to the House, where reports from the committee would then be offered, and then it goes to the House floor for a second reading. The bill may be debated at this point, and additional amendments may be offered. After a third reading on the House floor, the bill is put to a vote for final passage.

In the Senate, bills go through a similar process, after being introduced, assigned to the appropriate committees by the Senate President, undergoing hearings, debate and possible amendments. Following the second, and then third reading before the whole chamber, a final vote is taken for the bill's passage.

If a Senate bill passes without any amendments, it goes to the governor for his or her signature, otherwise it goes to a conference committee composed of three members of each chamber, where they will work out language acceptable to both houses. When a majority agrees, the conference committee report is submitted to both the House and Senate for an up or down vote.

All bills requiring funding must be sent to the appropriation committee, which adds a clause specific to the amount of spending. Once passed by the House and Senate, the bill becomes law when signed by the governor. If the governor fails to sign the bill within ten days while the General Assembly is in session, or after thirty days when it is out of session, that bill becomes law. If the governor vetoes the bill, a veto message must be sent to the General Assembly, and a 2/3 vote from each chamber can override the veto.

Colorado also has a process of referendum and initiative where citizens can petition to make changes to the constitution and existing statutes through the ballot box.

Appendix 1 presents a simple infographic describing the process whereby a federal bill becomes law.[17]

Legislative Activism

As mentioned, related to this area of inquiry, useful information for citizen activists interested in getting involved with the policy making process is widely available. Perhaps the most accessible and valuable collection of such resources is available from UN Women, an organization that has successfully organized legislative campaigns focusing on human rights and gender equality all over the planet.

While the agenda for this organization is specifically focused on women's rights issues, their extensive catalog of resources, publications and strategies would be useful for anyone seeking to promote any significant changes through the legislative process [see Appendix 2].

Their website can help citizen activists to get organized, and plan a sustained, effective legislative campaign, complete with blueprints for understanding who to meet, where and when to discuss substantive issues, and how to publicly promote the project for maximum effect.

Another venerable group that can assist in successfully navigating citizen driven legislation campaigns is the American Civil Liberties Union (ACLU). Their office in Nevada has produced the encompassing and informative Guide to Being an Effective Citizen Lobbyist, which can lead even novice activists step-by-step through the process, covering such topics as understanding the legislative process, becoming a citizen lobbyist, contacting legislators, participating in committee hearings, writing letters to the editor and more.[18]

Sociological Context for SOM

Another area of inquiry concerns the social contexts and historical background related to the development of the predominant correctional/punitive legal responses to sex offenders.[19,20]

In the late 1990's, around the beginnings of the contemporary era of SOM, J. Paul Fedoroff, one of Canada's foremost Forensic Psychiatrists, co-authored a very comprehensive, foundational study challenging the prevalent misconceptions and fallacies associated with sexually based offenders, and citing unfounded characterizations as major obstacles in developing more effective, realistic approaches in sex offender treatment. Among the most destructive myths and baseless stereotypes impacting how the public views this category of offender, Fedoroff lists the following:

> "...sex offenders are all socially deprived men; sex offenders are the result of childhood abuse; sex offenders shouldn't masturbate; sex offenders have too much testosterone; sex offenders can't be cured; sex offenders always lie to stay out of treatment; sex offenders are sex maniacs; public notification of sex offender release protects the community; sex offenders are all the same."[21]

Fedoroff's findings have been replicated again and again since first being published, with one of the more insightful studies being Sex Offender Myths in

Print Media: Separating Fact from Fiction in U.S. Newspapers, which employed content analysis to evaluate a sample of 334 articles published in over two thousand newspapers across the US for the presence of sex offender myths. The authors note the persistent mistaken beliefs about sex offenders that contradict findings supported by empirical research, such as identifying sex offenders as being compulsive, homogenous, specialists, and incapable of benefiting from treatment. "These myths," states the article, "affect the public's overall perception of sex offenders and their crimes, which, in turn, can influence public policy."[22] Moreover, Kaseweter presented clear findings that highlight the varied, diverse and complex, multifaceted characteristics of the highest-risk group of sexual offenders, again supporting Fedoroff's 1997 findings.[23]

Evidence-Based Therapeutic Practices

The third category of inquiry concerns the germane documentation about best practices and evidence-based results in psychology and behavioral science regarding the etiology, diverse characteristics and effective treatment of those who commit sexually based crimes.[24]

As the contemporary era of SOM continued developing through the 1990's and into the new millennium, a research article by Doris Layton MacKenzie, Evidence-Based Corrections: Identifying What Works, was eventually expanded into a book length treatise on the use of EBP with incarcerated offenders. Ms. MacKenzie was uncompromising in noting that "Relatively few policy decisions regarding corrections use scientific evidence to assist in making informed decisions." Her article, and later book, emphasized the importance of using evidence-based corrections for reducing crime and showed examples of how scientific information can be used to assess the effectiveness of correctional strategies, interventions, and programs.[25]

Early in the 21st Century, the American Psychiatric Association (APA) launched a presidential task force to define and describe evidence-based practices in psychology. That task force's report illuminated the full range of evidence that practitoners and policymakers must consider, stating that "EBP promotes effective psychological practice and enhances public health by applying empirically supported principles of psychological assessment, case formulation, therapeutic relationship, and intervention."[26]

Contrary to the EBP standards presented by the APA, and Doris Layton MacKenzie, SOM requirements in programs across the nation may include frequent lie detection sessions, as well as plethysmography to measure penile responses to visual and spoken stimuli, chemical castration, confessional journaling and correctional behavioral training, none of which have been proven to be effective treatments or preventative measures for ex-offenders.[27]

The same year the APA report was issued, Dr. William D. Murphy, professor of Psychiatry, at the University of Tennessee, in collaboration with Robert McGrath, Clinical Director of the Treatment Program for Sexual Abusers at the Vermont Department of Corrections, published a scholarly article entitled Best Practices in Sex Offender Treatment in the *Prison Service Journal.* Listing what they consider the minimum requirements for evidence based practices, including:

- Have a clear, evidenced-based model of change;
- Adhere to the risk, need, and responsivity principles, such that:
    - intensity of services is matched to risk (the risk principles);
    - treatment targets are chosen that are clearly linked to reoffending (need principle);
    - use effective methods, primarily, cognitive behavioral and skills based, and ensure treatment is adjusted to the learning style of the individual, and methods are designed to engage and motivate (responsivity principle);
- Ensure continuity of care;
- Provide staff appropriate training and supervision;
- Conduct ongoing program monitoring and evaluation.[28]

Those interested in getting actively involved in promoting EBP to legislators and other policy-makers, would do well to examine the progress made by the state of Colorado, where, as mentioned above, the legislature mandated the creation of a Sex Offender Management Board (SOMB) to oversee their state-run SOM programs. The official, description of the SOMB includes the following, "The board shall research, either through direct evaluation or through a review of relevant research articles, and sex offender treatment empirical data, and analyze, through a comprehensive review of evidence-based practices, the effectiveness of the evaluation, identification, and treatment policies and procedures for adult sex offenders."[29]

Literature Review

Scholarly research in the field of SOM appears to be slightly beyond the Nascent stage, not quite at the Intermediate stage, of the Scientific Continuum.[30] As such,

Seminal and Contextual literature are essential in gaining insight and understanding into developments in this field, as well as recent writings published within the past five years. The literature in this field indicates that most of the primary contemporary developments dominating current SOM practices began in the late 1990's and continue with characteristically similar practices into the present,[31] accompanied by similar misconceptions and commonly held fallacies about people who commit such crimes.[32,33] Some of the currently standard regulations and procedures include mandatory testing[34] and therapeutic interventions that are far from conclusive in terms of outcomes and intended results,[35,36] whereas promising, cutting edge therapeutic approaches are rarely included in the catalog of legal interventions incorporated in correctional settings or within post-incarceration parole and probation practices.[37]

Turning attention to the legislative process, the literature is abundant in this area, which can easily be classified as in the Mature stage on the Scientific Continuum. The internet, as well as library reference departments, contain numerous resources to help guide individuals through a detailed understanding of how proposals are introduced in law making bodies, and how those proposals then become statutes and regulations, such as The Legislative Process in Colorado.[38] The Colorado Division of Criminal Justice also offers extensive information detailing the SOM programs employed within that state, which, as mentioned, are considered among the most up-to-date, EBP treatment programs in the U.S, although still somewhat short of the mark.

Many options are available for citizen advocates who want to intervene in legal policy making deliberations. Scholarly literature in this area appears to be short of the Intermediate stage of the Scientific Continuum, as there has been some academic inquiry into these issues, but most of the resources seem to originate from activist organizations that target specific areas of advocacy, thereby limiting a more overarching and global perspective on such matters. As mentioned, one notable exception is the comprehensive information provided by U.N. Women in their web report, entitled Influencing Legislators or Other Policy Makers[39] which is designed to lead even novice activists through the complexities involved in getting their voices and agendas heard by all manner of legislative bodies large and small.

Conclusion

This chapter presented a good deal of substantive and authoritative material about the primary societal context driving the development and execution of SOM programs, as well as considerable evidence indicating the widespread endemic misinformation, myths and misunderstandings about the nature of these offenders, and their widely diverse behaviors and motives, in addition to offering information about evidence-based practices that challenge the dominant accepted correctional/punishment paradigm, and indicate the distinct potential for better, more effective, and improved outcomes in therapeutic and behavioral interventions with those convicted of sex crimes. The data presented here may be useful for psychotherapists and other professionals working with this category of offender, as well as beneficial to the offenders themselves, whose lives are burdened with regulatory requirements far beyond those of other types of felons.

Finally, this chapter offered some step-by-step, practical, hands-on guidance for individuals and groups who are interested in getting directly involved in changing the current state of SOM through advocating for revising current legal requirements and removing some existing interventions that are not backed up by scientifically empirical evidence.

ENDNOTES

1. Kus, 2015.
2. Lacombe, 2013.
3. CO.gov, 2018.
4. Laws & Marshall, 2003.
5. DiBennardo, 2017.
6. Huffman, 2015.
7. Lasher, et al, 2012.
8. Schiavone & Jeglic, 2009.
9. Huffman, 2015.
10. Liptak, 2017.
11. DiBennardo, 2017.
12. Rogers, 1957.
13. CO.gov, 2018.
14. Huffman, 2015.
15. UN Women, 2012.
16. Denver Republican Party 2009.
17. Votesmart.org, 2018.
18. ACLU, n.d.
19. Fedoroff & Moran, 1997.
20. Laws et al, 2003.
21. Fedoroff & Moran, 1997.
22. Galeste et al, 2012.
23. Kaseweter et al, 2016.
24. Malin & Saleh, 2014.
25. MacKenzie, 2009.
26. APA, 2008.
27. DiBennardo, 2017.

28. Murphy & McGrath, 2008.
29. CO.gov, 2018.
30. Edmonson & McManus, 2007.
31. Laws & Marshall, 2003.
32. Huffman, 2015.
33. Fedoroff & Moran, 1997.
34. Lacombe, 2015.
35. Bassler, 2016.
36. Malin & Saleh, 2014.
37. Roseman et al, 2009,
38. CO.gov, 2018.
39. U.N. Women, 2012.

REFERENCES

American Civil Liberties Union of Nevada, (n.d.), A guide to being an effective citizen lobbyist. Retrieved from https://www.aclunv.org/sites/default/files/a_guide_to_being_an_effective_citizen_lobbyist.pdf

American Psychiatric Association, (2006), Evidence-based practice in psychology: APA presidential task force on evidence-based practice. Retrieved from http://www.apa.org/pubs/journals/features/evidence-based-statement.pdf

Bassler, W., (2016), The effectiveness of sex offender treatment programs. Sex Offender Solutions and Education network. Retrieved from https://sosen.org/blog/2016/04/22/the-effectiveness-of-sex-offender-treatment- programs.html

Colorado.,gov/ Division of Criminal Justice (2018), Overview of sex offender management in Colorado: Understanding how Colorado classifies, supervises, and treats convicted sex offenders. Retrieved from https://www.colorado.gov/pacific/dcj/overview-sex-offender-management-colorado

Colorado.gov, (2018), The Legislative Process in Colorado. Retrieved from https://www.colorado.gov/pacific/sites/default/files/The%20Legislative%20Process_3.pdf

Colorado.gov, (2018), Sex offender management board. Retrieved from https://www.colorado.gov/pacific/dcj/sex-offender-management-board

Denver Republican Party, (2009), How a bill becomes law in Colorado. Retrieved from http://www.slideshare.net/denvergop/how-a-bill-becomes-law-in-colorado

DiBennardo, R., (2017), Sex offenders are among the most harshly punished criminals in the state, but how often does the punishment fit the crime? Retrieved from https://csw.ucla.edu/2017/01/05/sex-offenders-among-harshly-punished-criminals-state-often-punishment-fit-crime/

Edmonson, A.C., McManus, S.E., (2007), Methodological fit in management field research. Academy of Management Review 32(4)

Fedoroff, J.P., Moran, B., (1997) Myths and misconceptions about sex offenders, Retrieved from https://search-proquest-com.proxy.cecybrary.com/docview/220804813/77FEC1E0A5C446A3PQ/1?accountid=144789

Galeste, M.A., Fradella, H.F., Vogel, B., (2012), Sex offender myths in print media: Separating fact from fiction in U.S. newspapers. Retrieved from https://asu.pure.elsevier.com/en/publications/sex-offender-myths-in-print-media-separating-fact-from-fiction-in

Glasser, W. (2000). Reality therapy in action. New York, NY, US: HarperCollins Publishers. Retrieved from http://psycnet.apa.org/record/1999-04467-000

Hazler, Richard J., Counseling and Psychotherapy Theories and Interventions. Chapter 7: Person-Centered Theory. 6th Ed. 2016. American Counseling Association https://www.psychologytoday.com/us/therapy-types/person-centered-therapy

Huffman, M. K., (2015), The politics of fear: The dubious logic underlying sex offender registration statutes – proposals for restoring measures of judicial discretion to sex offender management, University of Nevada, Reno, ProQuest Dissertations Publishing, 2015. 1591360. Retrieved from https://search-proquest-com.proxy.

Kus, E. A., (2015), The relationship between sex offender legislation and psychosocial factors, The Chicago School of Professional Psychology, ProQuest Dissertations Publishing. Retrieved from https://search-proquest-com.proxy.cecybrary.com/

Lacombe, D., (2013) "Mr. S., you do have sexual fantasies?" the parole hearing and prison treatment of a sex offender at the turn of the 21st century. Canadian Journal of Sociology, Vol. 38 Issue 1, p33-63. 31p.

Lasher, M. P., McGrath, R. J., (2012), The impact of community notification on sex offender reintegration: a quantitative review of the research literature. Retrieved from https://search-proquest-com.proxy.cecybrary.com/docview/923242167/7CAA97176F8D4E4APQ/7?accountid=144789

Laws D.R., Marshall, W.L., (2003), A brief history of behavioral and cognitive behavioral approaches to sexual offender treatment: Parts 1 Early developments, and Part 2. The modern era. Retrieved from http://journals.sagepub.com/doi/abs/10.1177/107906320301500202?journalCode=saxb

Liptak, A. (2017), Did the supreme court base a ruling on a myth? Retrieved from https://www.nytimes.com/2017/03/06/us/politics/supreme-court-repeat-sex-offenders.html

MacKenzie, D.L., (2009), Evidence-Based Corrections: Identifying What Works. Retrieved from https://www.cambridge.org/core/books/what-works-in-corrections/D10E55C780D8BBF78FB0EDA19D6D1AD3

Malin, H.M., Saleh, F. M., (2014), The role of psychiatry in sex offender management. Retrieved from http://www.psychiatrictimes.com/special-reports/role-psychiatry-sex-offender-management

Murphy, W.D., McGrath, R., (2008), Best practices in sex offender treatment. Prison Service Journal #178. Retrieved from https://www.researchgate.net/publication/273760537_Best_practices_in_sex_offender_treatment

Rogers, Carl R. (1957). The Necessary and Sufficient Conditions of Therapeutic Personality Change. Journal of Consulting Psychology, 21. Retrieved from http://www.shoreline.edu/dchris/psych236/Documents/Rogers.pdf

Roseman, C.P., Ritchie, M., Laux, J.M., (2009), A restorative justice approach to empathy development in sex offenders: An exploratory study journal of addictions & offender counseling. Retrieved from https://search-proquest-com.proxy.cecybrary.com/docview/194445926/673F12169C4542C9PQ/2?accountid=144789

Schiavone, S. K., Jeglic, E. L., (2009), Public perception of sex offender social policies and the impact on sex offenders. International Journal of Offender Therapy and Comparative Criminology; London Vol. 53, Iss. 6:679 https://search-proquest-com.proxy.cecybrary.com/docview/197148993/F83EAC735B1140D9PQ/3?accountid=144789

UN Women webpage, (2012), Influencing legislators or other policy makers. Retrieved from http://www.endvawnow.org/en/articles/121-influencing-legislators-or-other-policy-makers-.html

Votesmart.org, (2018), How a Bill Becomes Law, https://votesmart.org/education/how-a-bill-becomes-law#.W5_roKZKjb0

Appendix 1 (Votesmart 2018)

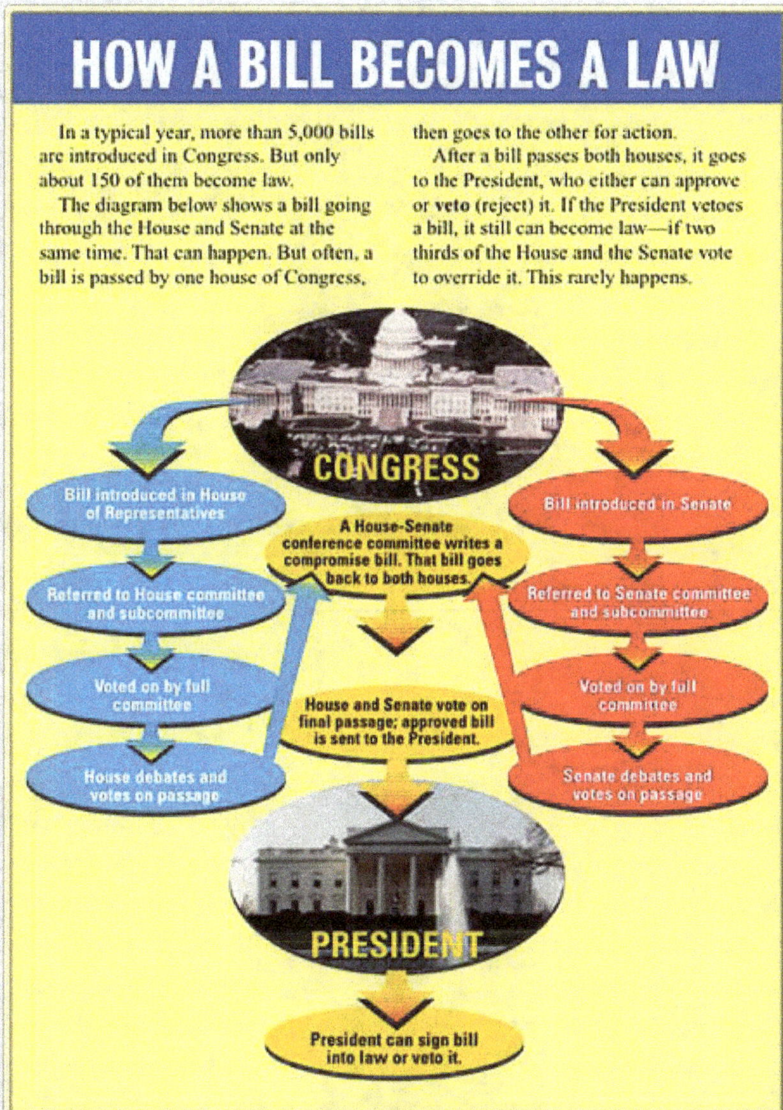

Appendix 2 (UN Women, 2013)

Individual Meetings or Briefings: A briefing is designed to present facts and analysis of proposed legislation to a group of parliamentarians and their staff whereas an individual meeting literally occurs with a single parliamentarian and possibly his/her staff.

In planning individual meetings, advocates should:

- Consider the most appropriate time to hold the meeting or briefing based on the schedules of the legislature and whether they are in session or not;
- Research where individual meetings and briefings are typically held – in the legislative office building or at the offices of an NGO – and consider the most appropriate location based on the message you want to convey;
- Determine what information will be highlighted in the meeting, the purpose of the meeting and the outcomes that are expected; and
- Send advance information – position paper, talking points, bill summary, etc. – but keep the information to a manageable length.

In planning briefings, advocates should:

- Make sure to invite the other NGOs and/or government officials well in advance – at least 5 to 6 weeks – and send a "Save the Date" message with the official invitation 3 to 4 weeks in advance of the briefing
- Make personal invitations to the meeting or briefing as appropriate and include the legislator's staff to attend.
- Research the position of the legislator or policy maker in advance of the meeting and anticipate questions and concerns.
- Develop and practice a concise and understandable three minute message.

16

Police Use of Force

antoniodiaz/Shutterstock.com

This chapter is presented in two different parts. The first piece offers a description and analysis of a 2010 landmark study by Klahm and Tillyer, Understanding Police Use of Force: A Review of the Evidence, including which parts of the study seemed to be the most enlightening, what additional information policy makers and police departments might like to have after reviewing the study to have a better understanding of addressing use of force standards, what significant facts from the study could be used for reformation or reduction of the local police use of force regulations, and what could be included in a new meta-analysis that might broaden the conclusions of the Klahm and Tillyer study.

The second part is an overview of contemporary trends, attitudes, and concerns regarding the use of force by US law enforcement personnel in the years since Klahm and Tillyer published their study, presented in a more journalistic approach to the subject matter, while still maintaining the same rigor of academic research.

Part 1

BRIEF DESCRIPTION AND ANALYSIS OF THE KLAHM AND TILLYER STUDY

At the time of the publication of their archival study in 2010, on the use of force by police in the U.S., Charles Klahm IV was a professor of Social Sciences at St. Joseph's College in New York,[1] and Rob Tillyer was a professor of Criminal Justice at the University of Texas, San Antonio.[2] According to their abstract, their article was the result of a collected analysis of almost two dozen previously published use of force studies culled from peer-reviewed journals published between 1995 and 2008.

The authors examined twenty-three different studies from which they extrapolated slightly more than two hundred distinct, independent variables that could serve to determine all the various elements involved in the use of force by police as reflected in the extant literature. However, due to space limitations they decided to constrain their discourse to only seventeen of the most commonly found variables represented in the material that they reviewed, divided into three characteristic categories, according to the qualities of the suspect, the officer and the encounter,[3] as described in Figure 1 below.

Variables	Positive relationship	Negative relationship	Mixed findings	No relationship	# of studies
Suspect characteristics					
Race/Ethnicity (minority)	2	--	7	8	17
Gender (male)	8	--	6	3	17
Age (older)	--	7	3	5	15
Demeanor	4	--	2	7	13
Social class (lower)	5	--	2	2	9
Intoxication	7	--	5	3	15
Encounter characteristics					
Weapon	4	--	5	1	10
Proactive contact	4	--	5	1	10
Resistance	8	--	1	1	10
Arrest	5	--	1	--	6
Other officers	3	1	4	2	10
Other citizens	1	--	3	8	12
Conflict	4	--	2	1	7
Officer characteristics					
Race (non-white)	--	--	2	9	11
Gender (Male)	2	--	3	10	15
Age	--	2	--	1	3
Experience	--	4	4	5	13
Education	--	2	2	1	5

Figure 1 [source: Klahm & Tillyer, 2010]

The authors explained that the time frame for the research literature they selected, 1995- 2008, was based upon a number of factors which they considered significant. One of the most important of these was a groundbreaking study, published in a 1995 edition of the *Criminal Justice Review*, which established a set of comprehensive academic definitions for the use of force, entitled Measuring The Continuum of Force Used by and Against the Police,[4] which Klahm and Tillyer expected to become a benchmark in setting law enforcement standards for such definitions into the future. The primary significance of the 2008 cut-off date is simply that's when the authors began gathering the material for their research, which was published two years later.[5]

While somewhat groundbreaking in its own right, the Klahm and Tillyer study is beset with several significant limitations, as noted by the authors themselves. One involves some of the known possible disadvantages inherent in archival research, including lack of control over how the original findings were gathered, whether the source research covered all pertinent key issues concerning the matter at hand, and whether any of the previous studies were up to the same standards that the archival researchers were aiming for.[6]

Additional possible disadvantages, as stated by the authors themselves several times in various contexts within the body of their study, concern the relative inconsistencies in the meaning and circumstances of the variables reported from one study to the next, including the very parameters required for uniform standards in defining "use of force." They note that, despite the establishment of suitable academic standards for this terminology with Garner, et al, in1995, as referred to above, there has been a persistent, widespread failure among scholars in this field to provide a consistent, universally accepted understanding of the use of force by police. Quoting the authors, "Even among those studies that provided definitions of force, the degree of specificity varies considerably." The authors had to navigate through widely differing descriptions of officer involved actions, where each report might include, or exclude, what may be key information, assign different levels of importance, if any, to circumstantial factors, such as location, time of day, gender, whether alcohol or drugs were involved, and so on, which all may be vital and essential factors for understanding what trends, if any, show up in police use of force incident reports.[7]

THE KLAHM & TILLYER STUDY AND LAW ENFORCEMENT POLICY

The inconsistencies mentioned above are among the reasons that the Klahm and Tillyer study might be difficult to utilize as a guidebook for law enforcement officials and policy makers seeking to address use of force standards and regulations. In addition, their study offers very little in the way of describing the specific sizes and composition of the various police departments who provided the source quantitative data, and in what manner the circumstances may vary from region to region, from cities to small towns, and other related pertinent factors.

Even with its somewhat limited scope, Klahm and Tillyer's study is still listed in a 2017 article, Five Use of Force Studies Cops Should Know, by veteran Colorado police chief, and founder of the National Center for Police Advocacy, Joel Shults, published in the nationwide online information exchange, PoliceOne, a professional service organization dedicated to sharing law enforcement related information and resources from officers and departments from across the United States and around the world.[8] While acknowledging similar inconsistencies and lapses that have been mentioned previously in each of the five studies he listed,

Shults agrees that more research of this kind is needed by law enforcement decision makers, and that the variables among the wide variety of department reports are too many to precisely define.[9]

One major step toward addressing some of these studies' various limitations may be the recent establishment of the first country-wide database, the National Use-of-Force Collection, devoted specifically to recording police use of force incidents, presumably offering greater consistency in the information collected, and thus able to present a fuller picture of trends across the U.S.A. than has been available to date.[10] Although participation in this database is not a requirement for all of America's law enforcement agencies, the FBI notes that the National Use-of-Force Collection resulted from the high number of requests from police officials across the country, and in fact, the FBI worked closely with professionals from a wide variety law enforcement agencies and establishments throughout the U.SA to develop the specific features and parameters of the data collection, and the FBI anticipates that involvement will be widespread enough to provide very meaningful results over time.[11]

IMPART OF THIS STUDY

While Klahm and Tillyer's findings may represent only a very small part of the overall picture of what kind of use of force events are happening in America's approximately 18,000 police agencies,[12] perhaps at its best, the study, as is, could provide a kind of template, or suggest a set of criteria that law enforcement executives and policy designers could use to determine the range of issues that individual departments would need to address in order to gain greater knowledge and oversight over their personnel's use of force.

Part 2

One of the most contentious hot-button topics in law enforcement today concerns the police use of force, underscored in recent years by several highly publicized cases, such as the deaths of George Floyd in Minneapolis MN, Breanna Taylor in Louisville KY, Michael Brown in Ferguson MO, and Tyre Nichols in Nashville TN. While incidents that result in the death of civilians may receive national, even international attention, there are many more, possibly thousands, of less-than-lethal events where the use of force has generated significant attention and scrutiny from local citizens, the media, and governmental entities.

In the 2016 book, *Shooting to Kill*, Oxford University professor Seumas Miller defines the law enforcement officer's (LEOs) role in terms of "protecting the legally enshrined, justifiably enforceable, moral rights of citizens from violation by fellow citizens, and the use of coercive, including lethal, force in pursuing this end." The International Association of Chiefs of Police (IACP) describes the use of force as "the amount of effort required by police to compel compliance by an unwilling subject."[13]

There are about 800,000 sworn LEOs in the US, including municipal police, county sheriffs, state troopers, and federal law enforcement agents. In their 2020 report, Overview of Police Use of Force, the National Institute of Justice (NIJ), states that situational awareness is essential, and all officers should be trained to judge when a crisis requires the use of force to gain the necessary control over a situation. Officers may receive some guidance from their individual agencies, but there are no universal regulations governing when or how much force LEOs should use.[14]

For all the attention and inquiries that this issue has generated, the US lacks a single authoritative database that details and tracks all use of force incidents, making it difficult to examine the actual prevalence, along with the specific reasons or consequences for the use of force.

A 2022 report from the Institute for Public Research at the Center for Naval Analyses noted that recent social movements calling for police reform in the use of force have highlighted the lack of data collected or publicly available on such incidents, accompanied by a lack of transparency and consistency on disciplinary processes and protections put into place. While the FBI attempted to launch a definitive database to track police use of force in 2017, voluntary reporting of such events by this nation's 18,000+ law enforcement agencies has been insufficient – about 14% responded -- leaving the FBI's database essentially ineffectual.[15]

Jason C. Johnson, head of the Law Enforcement Legal Defense Fund, told ABC News. "The lack of ability to have reliable and comprehensive data on police use-of-force is one of the biggest things that is hampering law enforcement's objective, which is really to gain the trust of the community. It is critical that we have thorough, comprehensive data about police use of force."

There are a number of alternative databases recognized as reliable and valid, such as the Pulitzer prize-winning WaPo Fatal Force Database, which has logged every deadly shooting in the United States by a police officer in the line of duty since 2015 and includes the federal IDs of the police departments involved. This database has logged nearly 8,000 fatal police shootings since its inception, uncovering an overall upward trend in the shootings and disputing federal records indicating fatal shootings by police have been declining nationwide since 2015. In 2021, The Post logged 1,047 fatal shootings, up 5% from the 994 fatal police shootings counted in 2015. A subsequent Post investigation found that the FBI undercounted fatal police shootings by more than half. In 2020, the Post database received recognition from the NYU School of Journalism as one of the top ten works of journalism of the decade, and in 2022, the database was honored with a Peabody Award.[16]

Statista provides another reliable and valid database tracking police use of force. Over 2,000 universities rely on Statista, including Harvard, Stanford, and Yale, as well as hundreds of industrial concerns around the world. Like the WaPo database, Statista also asserts that the trend of fatal police shootings in the United States seems to be increasing, with 1,096 fatal police shootings in 2022, up from 1,048 in 2021.[17]

Broadly speaking, the use of force by LEOs becomes necessary and is generally allowed only under specific circumstances, such as in self-defense or in defense of another individual or group. However, there is no single, universally agreed-upon definition of the use of force. Officers may receive guidance from their individual agencies, but no universal set of rules governs when LEOs should use force and how much. The IACP points out that situational awareness is essential, and officers should be trained to judge when a crisis requires the use of force to regain control of an event, but that training is not consistent from agency to agency.

One individual who has influenced the discussion concerning police use of force is Dave Grossman, author of *Bulletproof Mind*, a nationally prominent trainer who has endorsed the concept of LEOs as "warrior cops." A retired Army ranger and former West Point instructor, for the past two decades Grossman has conducted thousands of training events for law enforcement agencies in all 50 States: "If you properly prepare yourself, killing is just not that big a deal. Are you prepared to snuff out a human life in defense of innocent lives? If you can't make that decision, you need to find another job."

University of Nebraska Criminal Justice professor Samuel Walker has characterized Grossman's training as "okay for Green Berets but unacceptable for domestic policing."

In the 2013 book, *Rise of the Warrior Cop*, veteran NY Times journalist Radley Balko describes how a series of policies and relentless declarations of war against vague enemies like crime, drugs, and terror have blurred the distinction between cop and soldier. Balko documents how a creeping battlefield mentality has isolated and alienated many American police officers and put them on a collision course with the values of a free society. "Over the last several decades, America's cops have increasingly come to resemble ground troops. The consequences have been dire: the home is no longer a place of sanctuary, the Fourth Amendment has been gutted, and police today have been conditioned to see the citizens they serve as an 'other' -- an enemy."

"(LEOs) are taught that they live in an intensely hostile world. A world that is, quite literally, gunning for them," writes Seth Stoughton, a law professor, and former police officer, in a 2015 article for the *Harvard Law Review.* "Death, they are told, is constantly a single, small misstep away."[18]

In 2021, Brookings Technologies, renowned for its emergency vehicles and related products, issued a report comparing the mindsets of the *warrior cop* with the *guardian cop.* "The warrior mentality…often see police forces in military terms: they are soldiers fighting an enemy force, namely crime, as they try to uphold the law. The guardian mentality puts emphasis on protecting community members."

[see Chapter 2]

Wherever one comes down on the warrior/guardian debate, one thing is certain: the use of force is uniquely intrinsic to police work and will always be. That said, some 30 years ago, the UN Human Rights Commission, in their Eighth United Nations Congress on the Prevention of Crime and the Treatment of Offenders issued what they entitled the *Basic Principles on the Use-of-force and Firearms by Law Enforcement Officials:*

> "Law enforcement officials, in carrying out their duty, shall, as far as possible, apply non-violent means before resorting to the use-of-force and firearms…Law enforcement officials shall not use firearms against persons except in self-defense or defense of others against the imminent threat of death or serious injury, to prevent the perpetration of a particularly serious crime involving grave threat to life, to arrest a person presenting such a danger and resisting their authority, or to prevent his or her escape, and only when less extreme means are insufficient to achieve these objectives. In any event, intentional lethal use of firearms may only be made when strictly unavoidable in order to protect life."

This same concept is reflected in a more recent DHS update on the use of force policy following an executive order by President Joe Biden in March 2023: "LEOs may use force only when no reasonable, effective, safe and feasible alternative appears to exist and may use only the level of force that is objectively reasonable in light of the facts and circumstances confronting the LEO at the time force is applied."

ENDNOTES

1. Klahm, 2017.
2. UTSA, n.d.
3. Klahm & Tillyer, 2010.
4. Garner, J., et al, 1995.
5. Klahm & Tillyer, 2010.
6. Lentz, 2012.
7. Klahm & Tillyer, 2010.
8. Police Grants Help, 2022.
9. Shults, 2017.
10. FBI, 2018.
11. FBI, 2018.
12. Greenburg, E. 2016.
13. Miller, 2016.
14. NIJ, 2020.
15. CNA, Institute for Public Research..., 2022.
16. Washington Post Fatal Force Database, 2024.
17. Statista, n.d.
18. Stoughton, 2015.

REFERENCES

CNA Institute for Public Research, 2022, Sources For Police Use of Force Data. Retrieved from https://www.cna.org/our-media/indepth/2022/07/sources-for-police-use-of-force-data

FBI, (2018), FBI announces the official launch of the national use-of-force data collection. Retrieved from https://www.fbi.gov/news/pressrel/press-releases/fbi-announces-the-official-launch-of-the-national-use-of-force-data-collection

Garner, J., T. Schade, J. Hepburn and J. Buchanan. (1995). Measuring the continuum of force used by and against the police. Criminal Justice Review, Vol. 20, pp. 146 –168.

Greenberg, J., (2016), How many police departments are in the United States? Retrieved from https://www.politifact.com/punditfact/statements/2016/jul/10/charles-ramsey/how-many-police-departments-are-us/

Institute for Public Research at the Center for Naval Analyses (2022), retrieved from https://www.cna.org/our-media/indepth/2022/07/sources-for-police-use-of-force-data

Klahm, C., (2017), CV, Retrieved from https://people.wayne.edu/profile/eu2855/1578/klahm_cvoct_2017_.pdf

Klahm, C., Tillyer, R., (2010), Understanding police use of force: A review of the evidence. Southwest Journal of Criminal Justice, Vol. 7(2). pp. 214-23

Lentz, K, (2012), What are the advantages and disadvantages of using the archival method? Retrieved from https://www.enotes.com/homework-help/what-advantages-disadvantages-archival-method-332037

Miller, S., (2016) Shooting to Kill: The Ethics of Police and Military Use of Lethal Force, Oxford University Press, Oxford, England.

National Institute of Justice, 2020, Overview of Police Use of Force. Retrieved from https://nij.ojp.gov/topics/articles/overview-police-use-force

Police Grants Help.com, 2022, Your Resource for Police Department & Law Enforcement Grant Assistance. Retrieved from https://www.policegrantshelp.com/

Shults, J.F., (2017), 5 use of force studies cops should know. Retrieved from https://www.policeone.com/use-of-force/articles/416692006-5-use-of-force-studies-cops-should-know/

Statista (2024), retrieved from https://www.statista.com/statistics/585149/people-shot-to-death-by-us-police-by-gender/

Stoughton, S., (2015), Law Enforcement's "Warrior" Problem, retrieved from https://harvardlawreview.org/forum/vol-128/law-enforcements-warrior-problem/

UTSA College of Public Policy, (n.d.), Directory, Retrieved from http://copp.utsa.edu/criminal-justice/faculty-criminal-justice/

Washington Post Fatal Force Database (2024) retrieved from https://www.washingtonpost.com/graphics/investigations/police-shootings-database/

17

More Effective Police—Community Relations Through Media, Personal Engagement, and Collaborative Events

Dan Holm/Shutterstock.com

Introduction

The landmark 2015 Presidential Task Force on 21st Century Policing clearly indicates that one of the most effective ways to reduce crime in communities large and small is by improving the relationship between police personnel and the populations that they serve. According to a Rand Corporation study, the average American citizen tends to feel that their local police are generally not friendly, rude, and overly authoritarian.[1] This causes an abiding sense of disconnection, which adversely affects civilian willingness to inform local law enforcement about possible criminal activity, thereby negatively impacting the crime rates in that locality. The same Rand study asserted that by simply improving their communication style and finding ways to work together with local residents, those negative perceptions will be significantly reduced, which then leads to a corresponding decrease in crime. This paper further details these above-mentioned issues and provides accessible, simple, and effective solutions involving improvements in the manner in which law enforcement personnel communicate with their communities, as well as advancements in how citizens and cops can work together through a program of ongoing collaborations.

Making Connections

"Without trust between police and citizens, effective policing is impossible"[2]

Are you aware that local sporting events, jack-o-lanterns, and Christmas music, along with the focused use of public messaging and the media, can lead to less crime and an improved sense of community well-being?

Picture a late summer Sunday out at the Everytown municipal ballfield—it's the Constables versus the Dealership Gearheads for the local co-op league championship. Most of the town comes out for this game, as well as for the great B-B-Q extravaganza, which includes contributions from a half dozen of the best eateries in town. Always one of the biggest events every summer, it is not just the families or friends of the players who show up. And those unable to make it to the game can watch it live-streamed on the web or catch the replay on YouTube or over the local public access TV channel. A few months later, the annual Halloween pumpkin carving competition takes place in the high school parking lot, sponsored by several area law enforcement agencies as part of their yearly youth safety awareness campaign. This fun-filled contest, with prizes donated by local merchants, along with all sorts of sweets and treats, is also an opportunity to set up instructive displays, and info tables with exhibits and handouts, and other material relevant to this good cause. Then, nearing Christmas, it's the annual Cops & Kids choral program of holiday songs, usually one of the most well-attended concert performances of the year, with all the proceeds donated to a worthy aid organization selected by the community. Again, each one of these collaborative community events would also be live-streamed, and posted on the department's website, Facebook page, YouTube, over the public access TV channel, and so on.

As we will explore herein, research has revealed that the most effective sure-fire pathway to improving relations between law enforcement and the communities they serve is by creating collaborative events, coming together with a common purpose, and experiencing a shared sense of humanity.[3] The same research also indicates that the specific collective activities hardly matter—cooperating, communicating, and joining together are the most important elements. The possibilities for collaborative events are virtually endless.

While these kinds of shared community activities are important, they represent just one component of an overarching process that also includes ongoing public messaging through various media, along with a more approachable and friendly style of interaction between law enforcement personnel than civilians generally experience, where officers are seen as being approachable, and sociable[4] even when it's not a special holiday or sporting event.

As will be explained further on, these various tactics, along with others explored here, have been proven to help create a greater sense of trust between local law enforcement agencies and the citizens they serve, which then leads to less crime.[5] It also leads to a more positive sense of community, which tends to improve the quality of life and well-being of everyone involved.[6]

Community Policing Basics

The foundational concepts for creating more positive police/community relations are based upon the essentials of Community Policing, which first generated nationally widespread interest in the aftermath of the racial riots that spread across the US in the late 1960s and early 1970s.[7] In the years that followed, the United States Department of Justice (DOJ) has refined and codified the basics of Community Policing, culminating with the passage of the Violent Crime Control and Law Enforcement Act in 1994, and the formation of the Community Oriented Policing Services (COPS), designated by the DOJ as the agency responsible for advancing the practice of Community Policing through distributing information and funding grants to every level of America's law enforcement. In the years since, the need for effective strategies for better police/community relations has never been more front and center.[8]

2015 marks a defining landmark in understanding and advancing police-community relations with the publication of "The President's Task Force on 21st Century Policing Implementation Guide: Moving From Recommendations to Action". The task force was established by President Barack Obama to build trust between citizens and their law enforcement, in addition to other matters. Their final report provides a comprehensive accumulation of research revealing that various Community Policing procedures can unquestionably help reduce local crime rates by as much as 15%. The report also presents a wide range of policies and positive action steps that law enforcement agencies could undertake, in collaboration with their communities, to expand and support Community Policing.[9]

As a kind of companion piece to the President's Task Force report, "The Collaborative Toolkit for Community Organizations" is another one of COPS most useful contributions, offering a variety of innovative and effective step-by-step activities designed for citizens' groups who want to help advance better police/community relations.[10] It's fair to say that with just those two documents, any community could begin successfully establishing better police-community relations.

Culled from those and other relevant sources, what follows are some relatively simple and effective strategies for substantially enhancing police/community relations, through person-to-person contact and the purposeful use of mass media, straightforward measures that can be employed by any law enforcement agency, no matter the size, cultural makeup, or location.

Lest there be any misunderstandings, it's worth noting that before leaving office, President Donald Trump signed an executive order calling for legislation that would enhance existing federal grant programs to help police agencies grow community engagement,[11] underscoring that Community Policing is not some kind of far-left, anti-police agenda, and has nothing to do with many of the so-called defunding or dismantling strategies targeting law enforcement.

Evidence-Based Policing

Community Policing represents Evidence-Based Policing (EBP), which necessitates reconsidering long-standing attitudes toward traditional law enforcement tactics that may be prevalent but have no systematic evidence of effectiveness.[12] EBP requires that all agency policies and practices are proven to work and supported by substantial research. When conducted well and earnestly, Community Policing is measurably helpful in reducing crime and fostering better community relations.[13]

In their report, the President's Task Force recommendations covered these six topics

- Building Trust and Legitimacy
- Policy and Oversight
- Technology and Social Media
- Community Policing and Crime Reduction
- Officer Training and Education
- Officer Safety and Wellness

The President's Task Force on 21st Century Policing web page also includes links to video links capturing the various group discussions conducted by the task force members, a wide array of law enforcement, criminal justice, and public policy professionals, who gathered to delve into and contribute their expertise on these six topics. To understand the background, reasoning, and data supporting the report's practical findings more fully, those who are interested can review these videos.

As mentioned previously, among the most dramatic findings was that numerous locations practicing Community Policing saw up to a 15% decrease in crime, which some may consider reason enough to adopt the practice, even beyond the improved goodwill, social cohesion, and quality of life that can also result from Community Policing.

The focus here will primarily be on the topics of Building Trust and Legitimacy, Technology, and Social Media, along with the COPS topic of Collaborative Events.

That said, it is worthwhile to briefly touch upon the other Task Force topics insofar as they relate to more effective police-community relations. The Presidential Task Force research on Community Policing and Crime Reduction, already mentioned, detailed one of its most important findings, that at all levels and jurisdictions, locations that adopt Community Policing see their average crime statistics reduced, often dramatically.[14] Some of the reasons for this phenomenon will be discussed further on, as it relates to trust, fairness, and law enforcement personnel training, among the other topics, to be covered more fully here.

The subject of Policy and Oversight requires top local law enforcement executive personnel and their various jurisdictional lawmakers to get on the same page insofar as policing methods and procedures are concerned. For instance, certain "tough on crime" laws and mandates may impede a department's efforts in implementing Community Policing.[15]

In addition, elected officials may not be the only civilians with some authority over law enforcement policy and oversight. Beginning in the late 1940s and early 1950s, some communities across the US began to create civilian review boards to oversee police behavior[16] with an increase in the establishment of such boards across the county during the 1980s, including America's top 50 urban areas. Currently, about 200 such civilian review groups of some kind exist across the country, which is considerably fewer than the almost 1,000 or so such boards in the late 1980s.[17] There are voices pro and con, from the law enforcement and civilian camps, who hold widely divergent conclusions about the usefulness of such agencies, but currently, there is no standard for how to measure the effectiveness of police oversight by civilians, with such panels varying considerably in their structure and mandates.[18] One essential element of Community Policing is the need for well-defined, and transparent, departmental responses to officer misbehavior. Similarly, citizens should be well informed about the departmental standards required of every officer concerning their comportment and conduct, as this kind of general knowledge is a Community Policing must.[19]

Officer Safety and Wellness, as well as Officer Training and Education, are all intrinsic to a well-functioning Community Policing stratagem and deserve a much more expansive exploration on their own than space allows here. Briefly, the unique stresses of the job are known to take a toll, all too often dramatically so. In addition to group updates about the latest gear and tools of the trade, and effective responses to dangerous situations, officers should participate in regularly scheduled, comprehensive in-service training about self-care, and vicarious trauma, as well as undergo occasional mental and behavioral fitness evaluations. Inter-agency meetings concerning cooperation with and learning about significant civic and services organizations, in addition to relevant current location-specific crime trends, and other crucial current job-related subjects, should all be regularly covered.[20]

(see Chapter 4)

According to the DOJ's publication, "Police-Community Relations Toolkit: Policing 101", Community Policing training on average includes 11 hours on cultural diversity/human relations, eight hours on basic strategies, and eight hours on mediation skills/conflict management.[21] In addition, a Police Executive Research Forum (PERF) survey found that relatively few of the recruit and in-service training hours dedicated to use-of-force issues involve training on de-escalating potential use-of-force situations.[22] The lack of mental health crisis services across the U.S. has resulted in law enforcement officers serving as first responders to most crises. A Crisis Intervention Team (CIT) program is an innovative, community-based approach to improve the outcomes of these encounters. Of the 18,000 or so law enforcement agencies across the US, less than 3,000 communities nationwide have any critical incident training programs creating vital connections between law enforcement, mental health providers, hospital emergency services, and individuals with mental illness and their families.[23]

Building Trust and Legitimacy

Building trust starts with effective person-to-person communication.[24] Regardless of race, class, culture, or ethnicity, most law-abiding citizens generally only see police officers during a traffic stop, or when the officers are guarding something or someone, or during various official operations, or perhaps looking out from the inside of a patrol car—through dark glasses—seemingly distant, officious, and unfriendly.[25]

Due to the nature of the work, police officers usually engage in a linear style of communication, through giving orders or commands. This type of interaction is effective in dynamic situations or circumstances where an officer needs to gain compliance immediately, but it also eliminates factors that make interactions a more transactional two-way style of communication.[26]

A 2011 Rand Corporation study illuminated many considerations that affect a community's sense of trust and rapport with its local police personnel. These included such elements as body language, tone of voice and communication delivery style, perceived attitudes, presence—or lack of—empathy and understanding, and other such factors. Following these findings, the Rand study concluded that some departments need to address the often distant, impersonal, demanding demeanor of their police officers. This study also found that one of the easiest and most positive changes that patrol officers can make to generate goodwill is to simply step out of the patrol vehicles, take a walk through commercial and residential neighborhoods, and engage directly with the civilians in their communities.[27]

Very positive effects can happen with simple shifts in the tone of voice and content from rank-and-file officers. After some simple straightforward training, discussed in more detail later, law enforcement personnel can learn the basics of active listening and how to employ a more generally affable tone when conversing with the public. According to numerous studies, except for situations that require authoritative commands, citizens tend to hold more positive attitudes toward officers whose demeanor is friendly and conversational, thereby promoting increased citizen satisfaction in their interactions with police, which then leads to more civilian cooperation, a vital element in reducing crime, especially as people on the street often know more about what's going on in their neighborhood than law enforcement and will tend to avoid sharing that knowledge with officers they see as unfriendly.[28]

Active listening is a way of hearing and responding to another person that improves mutual understanding, as well as an essential first step for defusing tense situations and solving potential problems.[29] Active listening works for both parties in the conversation. It benefits the person speaking by helping to ensure that they are being heard, but it also benefits the listener by learning how to put distractions and preemptive judgments aside. Here are some examples of statements that officers could use to invite active listening:

"Let me see if I'm understanding you correctly..."

"So, what you're saying is..."

"Could you tell me a little more about that?"

"I'm sorry that you're going through that. How can I help?"

Sometimes simply restating what someone else has said, and maintaining eye contact with a friendly disposition can go a long way toward defusing an unnecessarily tense situation.[30]

When looking to create a sense of trust and legitimacy, the evidence shows that an officer's demeanor is very important, and a friendly, conversational tone helps citizens feel more trusting. It starts with considering how one communicates with the people they know, relatives, close friends, acquaintances and presenting the same kind of attitude, posture, and tone of voice, not at all like the officious armed warrior who seems ever wary of strangers.[31]

Collaborative Events

Research indicates that there may be some modest improvements in relations between police and minority communities through increased diversity in recruitment, and with programs like multicultural sensitivity and implicit bias training. However, by far the most well documented, evidence-based successes indicate that direct collaborations between police departments and local groups are the most reliable and effective way to improve relations between police and minority communities, providing the most durable, lasting, and positive results. *Any* type of collaboration—neighborhood watch, inter-agency sporting events, street fairs, citizen review boards, etc.—markedly improves police/community relations.[32]

The National Night Out, a widely observed annual mid-summer community-oriented event across the USA, provides an excellent opportunity to initiate ongoing collaborations between a local law enforcement agency and its community. Administered by the National Association of Town Watch (NATW), the National Night Out was launched in 1984 by the US DOJ's Bureau of Justice Assistance and was held in 400 communities involving 2.5 million people. It has since expanded to over 9,500 communities with some 32 million participating.[33] This program strengthens partnerships between communities and their police through a wide variety of activities within a festive atmosphere, including food stalls, water balloon toss competitions, face painting, tug-of-war contests, scavenger hunts, and so on.[34]

National Night Out is a perfect way to kick off a progression of cooperative ventures between law enforcement and the public going forward—but if that single once-a-year festival is the only collaborative event that the police and the citizens take on, it would not be nearly enough to support a successful Community Policing program, which would require various ongoing cooperative ventures large and small.

Important additional long-term collaborations should include regular sit-down meetings, one or two per month, between law enforcement personnel and representatives of various civic organizations, such as the Rotary, Lions, downtown merchants' associations, minority advocacy groups, interfaith alliances, parent-teacher organizations, and so on.[35] Such meetings help promote regular and dependable connectivity between the department and the civilians, while also providing an exchange of more information about comings and goings in the community that law enforcement may not otherwise know about, including burgeoning challenges, such as newly identified trends in criminal behavior, novel illegal substances showing up, or dangerous newcomers,[36] which is a large part of how Community Policing helps reduce crime.

Similarly, regular ongoing community-wide meetings, perhaps a half dozen per year, in large gathering places such as gymnasiums, auditoriums, and outdoor venues, can provide opportunities to meet face-to-face with the general public. Police officials and other public personnel could discuss concerns about developing criminal trends, responses to local catastrophes and other community-wide issues, as well as significant departmental policy changes, and so on. An open microphone could provide community participants the opportunity to ask questions or share comments as well, helping citizens to feel that they are being included and considered in the process.[37]

Such meetings could also be live streamed over a dedicated department website, and on Public Access TV, as well as posted to YouTube, as mentioned previously, and discussed in detail further on.

Many successful and effective police-community collaborations involve sports. The Police Athletic League (PAL) has long been known to foster positive community relations, especially with the younger populace.[38] Many communities host inter-agency competitions on the baseball field, hockey rink, basketball court, and so on—law enforcement personnel against other public agencies and civilian groups—firefighters, school teachers, fraternal orders, etc.[39] Golf shoot-outs, bowling tournaments, swim meets, track and field events. The possibilities are endless.[40]

Music shows up around the world as another successful way that communities have joined with their local law enforcement.[41,42] From choral collaborations during Christmas and other seasonal concerts, to bluegrass, country, and rock'n'roll jam sessions, hip-hop events, drum circles, talent showcases, and full-out festivals, few things can bring people together quite like music.[43,44]

In 2017, a Carnegie Hall ensemble group in NYC, Decoda, launched a musical collaboration between young people and cops in the wake of community protests and targeted shootings of police. The mission was to start a dialogue and after weeks of collaborating and performing together both the officers and the students felt that they could bring what they've learned back to their communities, and hopefully change some perspectives.[45]

Technology and Social Media

The current state of communication technology provides endless opportunities for police agencies to maintain a media presence, which is instrumental for successful Community Policing and offers far more engagement than just an occasional press release or Critical Incident report.[46]

The internet offers the prospect of ongoing communication with the public through mass emails, web pages, blogs, podcasts, live-streaming videos, and a wide array of social media, such as Facebook, Instagram, Tik Tok, and so on. Add to that traditional broadcast platforms like radio and TV, print media, and live events.

For effective Community Policing, handling the press, social media, and other communication technology, as well as public relations, calls for a Public Information Officer (PIO), someone who can oversee, coordinate, and help generate whatever messages are to be disseminated to the public, as well as to determine the most effective means to get it all out there. Among their most important duties, the PIO is responsible for the release of incident-related information involving important crimes and evolving situations, in addition to regular ongoing public relations.[47]

Although there are approximately 18,000 law enforcement agencies in the US,[48] according to the authoritative career site Zippia, there are only about 1,300 PIO's.[49] Some jurisdictions, especially in localities with agencies that receive funding from the US Department of Homeland Security, require that a PIO be on the staff, especially as the point person who is designated to report on Critical Incidents. However, it seems that most law enforcement agencies have decided a PIO is not necessary, for whatever reasons. If one of those reasons is budget constraints, the DOJ's Office of Community Oriented Policing Services (COPS) regularly awards grants to hire Community Policing professionals, such as PIOs. COPS also funds innovative policing approaches, especially related to Community Policing, providing training and technical assistance to community members, local government leaders, and all levels of law enforcement.[50]

The PIO may be a hands-on person with a media or internet background adept at handling most of the communication channels, or someone who is able to collaborate with people who have more expertise in handling equipment, pushing the buttons, or designing apps.

Many agencies have developed web pages dedicated to presenting up-to-date information on everything from local crime stats to departmental promotions to upcoming community-police collaborations. The city of San Diego's police department is an exemplary example and can be viewed at https://www.sandiego.gov/police. Internet presence can also be enhanced by posting relevant content through social media connections such as Facebook, Instagram, YouTube, and other popular platforms, in addition to presenting more in-depth information through podcasts. Live streaming on video is also available, which is detailed further on.

Two of the most available and generally underused media outlets are local radio and TV news, and PEG Television, also known as Community Access TV. There are over 15,000 commercial radio stations operating across the US, as well as some 1,500 Low Powered FM (LPFM) community-based radio stations.[51] There are also over 5,000 Public, Educational, and Governmental, or PEG, access TV channels across America.[52]

Local radio and TV newsrooms are always hungry for material to use on air. Utilizing radio to consistently communicate with the community can be as simple as issuing regular press releases on issues of interest, whether it be about newsworthy law enforcement stories, or public events related to upcoming community-police collaborations, or interesting developments within the agency.[53]

Local TV news is especially useful for announcing or promoting significant community-police-related events, as well as having LE officials appear as guests related to evolving events or Critical Incidents. While local television news programming may have shed some of its audience over the past decade, it still garners more viewers on average than cable and network news programs.[54]

Community Access or PEG TV, not to be confused with Public Television, is a non-for profit nation-wide system of channels mandated by federal law to be available free of charge, and can be utilized by police agencies in a wide variety of ways, from appearing as a guest on an already existing program to developing and producing original programming, which is not as complicated as it may seem at first.[55]

The P in PEG is for Public Access, which provides a free outlet for local citizens to create and distribute not-for-profit TV programming to the community, whether it be a single show, or an ongoing series, through pre-recorded videos, or live events. The types of programming shown on a community access channel vary by station.

The E in PEG is for Educational-access television, set aside for educational departments and organizations within the locality. Educational-access television channels may be associated with specific educational institutions, school districts, or even private organizations that are contracted to operate the educational-access television channel for the city (https://en.wikipedia.org/wiki/Public-access_television#cite_ref-13).

The G stands for Government-Access Television (GATV), a resource used by many governmental agencies to address developing local issues, present live legislative meetings, election programming, local emergency announcements, and so on.

In some community surveys, PEG access TV frequently fares as well or better in viewership compared to its commercial cable and network counterparts and frequently receives a 1% to 2% viewership share as compared with premium pay television and hundreds of cable channels that receive far less.[56]

Conclusions

As detailed in the aforementioned recommendations presented here, based on the President's Task Force following these simple guidelines to develop more effective police-community relations in jurisdictions of any size or cultural complexity, can significantly help prevent and reduce crime. Such an undertaking requires active listening and a generally sociable communication style from local law enforcement personnel. It will also require regular, ongoing meetings and direct engagement between the police and a wide variety of community organizations. There should also be numerous different types of collaborations planned throughout the year between the local law enforcement agencies and the citizenry, through various activities such as sports, PEG-TV productions, internet/social media presentations, musical partnerships, and seasonal events, as exemplified by the National Night Out. Funding, guidance, and complete information to launch such an endeavor is available through the Community Oriented Policing Services, and further details can be acquired through the Final Report of the Presidential Task Force on 21st Century Policing.

ENDNOTES

1. Rand, 2011.
2. Bureau of Justice Assistance 1994.
3. McCampbell, 2014.
4. Rand, 2011.
5. Reisig, 2007.
6. Alpert, et al, 2001.
7. Bureau of Justice Assistance 1994.
8. Norwood, 2020.
9. COPS, 2015.
10. US-DOJ, n.d.
11. Norwood, 2020.
12. Sherman, 1998.
13. Bullock & Tilley, 2016.
14. Office of Community Oriented Policing Services, 2015.
15. Johnson, 2017.
16. Center for Public Integrity, 2020.

17. Reasons, n.d.
18. NACOLE, 2016.
19. UNODC, 2011.
20. IACP, n.d.
21. US DOJ Community Relations Service, n.d.
22. PERF, 2015.
23. NAMI, 2022.
24. Conley, 2015.
25. Rand, 2011.
26. Loving, 2014.
27. Rand, 2011.
28. Johnson, 2016.
29. Milofsky, n.d.
30. Loving, 2014.
31. Milofsky, n.d.
32. McCampbell, 2014.
33. NATW, n.d.
34. PlanIt Police, 2017.
35. COPS, 2014.
36. McCampbell, 2014.
37. McCampbell, 2014.
38. COPS, 2020.
39. UNODC, n.d.
40. MacIntosh, 2017.
41. Oakdale Leader, 2022.
42. Guilfoil, 2021.
43. Scottish Police & Community Choir, 2021.
44. Maslov, 2019.
45. Duncan, 2017.
46. COPS, 2016.
47. Roberts, 2019.
48. Kershner, 2020.
49. Zippia, 2021.
50. Wilson, et at, 2014.
51. Vogt, 2016.
52. FCC, n.d.
53. Zercoe, 2015.
54. Pew Research Center, 2021.
55. FCC, 2020.
56. American Community Television, n.d.

REFERENCES

Alpert, G. P., Flynn, D., & Piquero, A. I. (2001). Effective community policing performance measures. Retrieved from https://scholarcommons.sc.edu/cgi/viewcontent.cgi?article=1008&context=crim_facpub

American Community Television. (n.d.). Retrieved from https://wcm.memberclicks.net/assets/docs/Library

Bullock, K., & Tilley, N. (2016). Evidence-based policing and crime. Retrieved from http://policing.oxfordjournals.org

Bureau of Justice Assistance, 1994, Understanding Community Policing: A Framework for Action. Retrieved from https://www.ojp.gov/pdffiles/commp.pdf

Center for Public Integrity. (2020). The long battle for civilian oversight of the police. Retrieved from https://publicintegrity.org/inequality-poverty-opportunity/the-long-battle-for-civilian-oversight-of-the-police/

Chen, N. (2019). D.C. police's side by side band uses music to connect to community. Retrieved from https://wjla.com/features/hero-247/side-by-side-dc-police-revive-70s-band-using-music-to-connect-to-the-community

Chequer, M. (n.d.). Exeter police and community choir. Retrieved from https://www.bbc.co.uk/programmes/p06rhtv7

College of Policing. (2020). Integrity and transparency. Retrieved from https://www.college.police.uk/What-we-do/Ethics/integrity-and-transparency/Pages/Integrity-and-Transparency.aspx

Conley, R. (2015). The 10 commandments of communication to build trust. Retrieved from https://leaderchat.org/2015/08/27/the-10-commandments-of-communication-to-build-trust/

Community Oriented Policing Service (COPS) Community Policing Dispatch. (2020). Police youth programs: Much more than fun and games. Retrieved from https://cops.usdoj.gov/html/dispatch/03-2020/youth_programs.html

Duncan, J. (2017). Officers and teens come together through music. Retrieved from https://www.cbsnews.com/news/officers-and-teens-come-together-through-music/

Federal Communications Commission (FCC). (2015). Public, Educational, and Governmental access channels ("PEG Channels"). Retrieved from https://www.fcc.gov/media/public-educational-and-governmental-access-channels-peg-channels

Federal Communications Commission (FCC). (n.d.). Public, Educational, and Governmental (PEG) access channels. Retrieved from https://transition.fcc.gov/osp/inc-report/INoC-7-PEG-Access-Channels.pdf

Guilfoil, J. (2021). Irish-American Police Officers Association presents a night of Traditional-Irish music. Retrieved from https://jgpr.net/2021/12/13/irish-american-police-officers-association-presents-a-night-of-traditional-irish-music/

International Association of Chiefs of Police (IACP). (n.d.). Officer safety and wellness. Retrieved from https://www.theiacp.org/resources/document/officer-safety-and-wellness

Johnson, R. R. (2017). Community policing is not soft on crime: The evidence. Retrieved from https://www.dolanconsultinggroup.com/wp-content/uploads/2017/08/ResearchBrief_CommunityPolicing.pdf

Johnson, R. (2016). Why officer demeanor matters. Retrieved from https://www.dolanconsultinggroup.com/wp-content/uploads/2016/08/Research_Brief_Why-Officer-Demeanor-Matters_August- 2016.pdf

Kershner, E. (2020). The largest police departments in the US. Retrieved from https://www.worldatlas.com/articles/the-largest-police-departments-in-the-us.html

Loving, K. (2014). Three ways for law enforcement to improve public-relations and trust. Retrieved from https://www.criminaljusticedegree.com/3-ways-for-law-enforcement-to-improve-public-relations-and-trust/

MacIntosh, A. (2017). Sports serve as tool to improve police-community relationships. Retrieved from https://risetowin.org/perspectives/2017/6-5/sports-serve-as-tool-to-improve-police-community-relationships/index.html

Maslov, E. (2019). NYPD officer and DJ: Community policing through music. Retrieved from https://www.voanews.com/a/nypd-officer-and-dj-community-policing-through-music/4759821.html

McCampbell, M. S. (2014). The collaboration toolkit for community organizations: Effective strategies to partner with law enforcement. Retrieved from https://rems.ed.gov/docs/COPS_CollaborationToolkit_CommunityOrgs.pdf

McCampbell, M. S. (n.d.). The collaboration toolkit for community organizations: Effective strategies to partner with law enforcement. Retrieved from htttps://ric-zai-inc.com/Publications/cops-p192-pib.pdf

Milofsky, A. (n.d.) United States Institute of Peace. What is active listening? Retrieved from https://www.usip.org/public-education/educators/what-active-listening

National Alliance on Mental Illness. (2022). Retrieved from https://www.nami.org/Advocacy/Crisis-Intervention/Crisis-Intervention-Team-(CIT)-Programs

National Association for Civilian Oversight of Law Enforcement. (2016). Building public trust through law enforcement accountability and transparency. Retrieved from https://www.nacole.org/benefits

National Association of Town Watch. (n.d.) About national night out. Retrieved from https://natw.org/about/

Northwestern University Graduate Program Staff. (2016). 3 ways ethics influence criminal justice. Retrieved from https://www.northeastern.edu/graduate/blog/3-ways-ethics-influence-criminal-justice/

Norwood, C. (2020). Calls for reform bring renewed focus to community policing, but does it work? Retrieved from https://www.pbs.org/newshour/politics/calls-for-reform-bring- renewed-focus-to-community-policing-but-does-it-work

Oakdale Leader. (2022). Music helps officers, community connect. Retrieved from https://www.oakdaleleader.com/news/music-helps-officers-community-connect/

Office of Community Oriented Policing Services. (n.d.). Law enforcement best practices. Retrieved from https://cops.usdoj.gov/RIC/Publications/cops-w0875-pub.pdf

Office of Community Oriented Policing Services. (2015). The president's task force on 21st century policing implementation guide: Moving from recommendations to action. Washington, DC: Office of Community Oriented Policing Services.

Oklahoma City Police Department. (2021). Community outreach: Jamming hoops fest. Retrieved from https://www.okc.gov/departments/police/community-outreach

Pew Research Center. (2021). Trend and facts on local TV news. Retrieved from https://www.pewresearch.org/journalism/fact-sheet/local-tv-news/

PlanIt Police. (2017). 10 National Night Out activities everyone will participate in. Retrieved from https://www.planitpolice.com/blog/national-night-out-activities-everyone-will-want-to-participate-in.2017

Police Athletic League. (2019). NYPD police officers and police athletic league youth performed original songs with Decoda at Pal Harlem Center Concert. Retrieved from https://www.palnyc.org/press/2019/2/27/nypd-police-officers-and-police-athletic-league-youth-performed-original-songs-with-decoda-at-pal-harlem-center-concert

Police Executive Research Forum (PERF). (2015). Re-engineering training on police use of force. Retrieved from https://www.policeforum.org/assets/reengineeringtraining1.pdf

Rand National Security Research Division (Treverton, G., Wollman, M., Wilke, E., & Lai, D.). (2011). Moving toward the future of policing. Retrieved from https://www.rand.org/content/dam/rand/pubs/monographs/2011/RAND_MG1102.pdf

Reasons, C. E. (n.d.). Citizen review: Civilian oversight board. Retrieved from https://www.britannica.com/topic/citizen-review

Reisig, M. D. (2007). What shapes residents' willingness to participate in crime prevention programs? *Policing: A Journal of Policy and Practice, 1*(3), 356-369.

Roberts, M. (2019). Public information officer job description. Retrieved from https://www.jobhero.com/job-description/examples/marketing/public-information-officer

Scottish Police & Community Choir. (2021). About us. Retrieved from https://policechoir.com/about-us/

Sherman, L. W. (1998). Evidence-based policing. Retrieved from https://www.policefoundation.org/wp-content/uploads/2015/06/Sherman-1998-Evidence-Based-Policing.pdf

Statista. (2020). Number of commercial radio stations in the United States from 1952 to 2020 Retrieved from https://www.statista.com/statistics/252235/number-of-commercial-radio-stations-in-the-us/

United Nations Office on Drugs and Crime (UNODC). (n.d.). Crime prevention through sports. Retrieved from https://www.unodc.org/dohadeclaration/en/topics/crime-prevention-through-sports.html

United Nations Office on Drugs and Crime. (2011). *Handbook on police accountability, oversight and integrity*. Retrieved from https://www.unodc.org/pdf/criminal_justice/Handbook_on_police_Accountability_Oversight_and_Integrity.pdf

US Department of Justice Community Relations Service. (n.d.). Police-community relations toolkit: Policing 101. Retrieved from https://www.justice.gov/file/1376626/download

Vogt, N. (2016). Number of U.S. low-power FM radio stations has nearly doubled since 2014. Retrieved from https://www.pewresearch.org/fact-tank/2016/09/19/number-of-u-s-low-power-fm-radio-stations-has-nearly-doubled-since-2014/

Wilson, Jeremy M., and Alexander Weiss. 2014. A Performance-Based Approach to Police Staffing and Allocation. Washington, DC: Office of Community Oriented Policing Service

Zercoe, C. (2015). Why police agencies should embrace news media. Retrieved from https://www.police1.com/pulse-of-policing/articles/why-police-agencies-should-embrace-news-media-otVLxmhGRk659O7j/

Zippia. (2021). Public information officer statistics by gender. Retrieved from https://www.zippia.com/public-information-officer-jobs/demographics/

18

Simple Self-Care Methods for Law Enforcement Personnel to Address Anxiety, Stress, Depression and PTSD

FotoDuets/Shutterstock.com

Alan Budman/Shutterstock.com

Antonio Guillem/Shutterstock.com

Introduction

Beyond the wide variety of unique situations and circumstances related to working in law enforcement, police are also subject to a full range of mental and emotional health concerns just like everyone else. However, in addition to facing all the risk factors, stressors and difficult life situations as other individuals, LEOs (law enforcement officers) usually encounter more demanding situations than the general public, often resulting in considerably more anxiety and stress. For example, according to the Illinois Criminal Justice Information Authority, police officers exhibit higher rates of PTSD than the rest of the population.[1]

Due to a combination of insufficient awareness about these issues, along with agency inattention, and some of the traditions of 'cop culture' -- such as an abiding sense that officers must uphold a tough-guy image — far too often LEOs fail to recognize or acknowledge the anxiety, stress, depression and PTSD they may be experiencing. However, there are wide variety of simple, do-it-yourself methods scientifically proven to be effective in reducing and even eliminating such problematic emotional, mental and physical conditions, which are easy to do, and can be performed at one's own pace individually, or in group settings, ideally with the support of their law enforcement agencies.[2]

The following includes several simple, evidence-based, self-care techniques. Interested readers will find much more information in the reference section at the end of this chapter, which can help lead to a less stressful existence. Just because one may work as a police officer doesn't mean that life has to feel like living inside a pressure cooker.

A Variety of Challenging Conditions for LEOs

According to the Law Enforcement Officer Fatalities Report of 2021, 458 federal, state, tribal and local officers died in the line of duty, while suicide claimed another 150 officers as well.[3] The CDC reports that police personnel are 54% more likely to commit suicide than the average American.[4] It is also estimated that 18-24% of police dispatchers, who are generally civilians, in addition to 35% of LEOs, suffer from PTSD—Post Traumatic Stress Disorder,[5] which may show up as chronically tense muscles, frequent headaches, faster than normal breathing, increased heart rate, uncontrollable trembling and sweating, a general feeling of weakness and tiredness, difficulty sleeping, and a frequently upset stomach or nausea.[6] As a result, many first responders turn to alcohol, drugs, and other destructive, self-damaging behaviors in an effort to cope with the stresses and problems they deal with on a regular basis.[7]

Anxiety is another issue that LEOs tend to encounter at a significantly higher rate,[8] generally characterized as feelings of tension and worried thoughts, which may be accompanied by increased blood pressure, sweating, trembling, dizziness, rapid heartbeat, and might include recurring intrusive threatening thoughts and fears. According to the American Psychological Association, some degree of anxiety is common for most people, but it is considered a serious disorder if it persists for longer than six months. Severe medical problems can result from long-term anxiety, including diabetes and heart irregularities. Over 40 million American adults have ongoing anxiety, with 30% experiencing clinical anxiety disorders,[9] and the rate for LEOs is higher than the civilian population.[10]

Related to anxiety, stress is a common biological response that, if persistent, can cause physical, emotional, or psychological strain, often as the result of circumstances that require extreme concentration, arduous activity, and the presence of bodily threats,[11] such as police work. Everyone experiences such pressures occasionally, however, LEOs are likely to encounter persistent stress more frequently, which can create a negative impact their well-being.[12] A World Health Organization report notes that trying to ignore stress often leads to significant mental and physical problems.[13] In 2022, 76% of US adults reported various ongoing impacts from stress, including headaches, fatigue, nervousness, and sadness. In addition, persistent anxiety and stress are also related to chronic conditions, such as gastro-intestinal issues, heart disease, migraines, and sleep problems.[14] Again, LEOs are more prone to such effects than the general population.[15]

Everyone gets sad from time to time, but persistent melancholy, with constant feelings of downheartedness and detachment, can develop into a major depressive disorder. The National Institute of Mental Health reported that 21 million Americans had at least one major depressive episode in 2022, and 2/3 of those developed a severe, persistent condition.[16] Depression often leads to sleep disruptions, heart disease, unhealthy weight fluctuations, a weakened immune system, and even physical pain.[17] According to a study reported in the International Journal of Emergency Mental Health and Human Resilience, LEOs are about twice as likely to suffer from depression as the rest of the population.[18]

In 2011 the International Association of Chiefs of Police issued their Critical Incident Stress Management Concepts and Issues Paper, alerting the law enforcement community of the extent of these problems and calling for a widespread response. While some law enforcement agencies have been taking steps to address these significant issues, there is much more that the 18,000+ departments across the US can do through a number of fairly simple, evidence-based practices that have long been shown to be highly effective in addressing anxiety, stress, and depression, all of them easy to do, and all scientifically substantiated. Through regular practice, improvements in one's mental and emotional state, as well as a significant reduction in anxiety, stress and depression, are highly likely-- and less stressed LEOs would certainly be a benefit to the civilians they serve as well.[19]

The Healing Power of Trees

In the 1930s, educator Kurt Hahn proved that by simply getting out and spending time in nature we can improve our physical, mental, and emotional health, with such activities as walking in the woods, camping out, or just being immersed in a physically beautiful environment. Hahn's findings have since been upheld by numerous scientific studies over the years and led to the creation of Outward Bound, a highly successful remedial program designed for youth at risk.[20]

The Japanese practice called Shinrin-yoku (Forest Bathing) includes hugging trees, listening to birds singing, and kicking through leaves, all proven to boost mental health. Trees also emit phytoncides, chemicals that can help boost our immune system. Such forest therapy is also becoming a recognized remedy throughout the world, supported by a number of scientific studies that confirm its beneficial effects, just as Kurt Hahn established in the 1930s.[21,22]

Yoga and Mindfulness

Some 3000 years ago, people in Southern Asia began developing the simple relaxation and mindfulness techniques of yoga, and their beneficial effects have been well established by modern science.[23] Numerous in-depth studies since the 1970s have further illuminated how yoga can promote a sense of well-being while improving physical health, and reducing tension and stress, thereby enriching our psychological and emotional state.[24] Mental, behavioral, and physical health practitioners worldwide routinely prescribe similar techniques, to treat anxiety, stress, and depression.[25] Yoga does not require any special physical prowess or stamina and could easily be learned from books or video clips. However, to be certain of correct posture alignments, an introductory yoga class or two is advised.[26]

Mindfulness is a related practice that has also been extensively studied and proven to be effective.[27] This involves comfortably sitting or lying down and purposely centering one's attention on the present moment. By focusing on the here and now, those who regularly practice mindfulness are less likely to worry, feel anxiety, or have regrets. Harvard studies, among others, have proven that mindfulness can be highly effective in reducing stress, lowering blood pressure, relieving chronic pain, and improving sleep. Again, a formal class or two is advisable to start off.[28]

Walking with Purpose

Arguably one of the easiest, most accessible exercises for addressing anxiety is brisk walking, which is described as an energetic stride with some exertion, but not quite running – and swinging the arms boosts the positive effects. This has been proven to be especially effective when done in a heavily wooded area for the added benefit of being surrounded by trees (see above),[29] however, even in urban environments, the confirmed benefits of brisk walking for about 40 minutes daily include stress relief, improved sleep and increased calm, among other healthy outcomes.[30]

Deep Relaxation

Deep relaxation is even easier than walking, as it involves no physical movement at all -- although beginners may need to learn how to stay awake. This exercise involves lying on one's back upon a comfortable surface, with arms and legs slightly apart, and then consciously relaxing each part of the body as completely as possible, from the tips of the toes up through to the top of the head, while staying fully awake and aware.[31] After becoming comfortable with the protocol, it is possible to relax one's entire body at will within seconds. The benefits of deep relaxation have also been well established by science.[32]

Humming

Of all the simple techniques presented here, humming may seem the least likely method to produce meaningful results, however, as reported by the Mayo Clinic and elsewhere, the scientific evidence is substantial and conclusive. Even just five minutes of continual humming is much more than just a self-soothing sound, as it can also reduce stress, induce calmness, and enhance sleep, as well as lower the heart rate and blood pressure while boosting beneficial neuro-chemicals that elevate mood… and no particular musical or vocal skills are required.[33,34]

Caffeine, Sugar, Alcohol and Drugs

Another element of self-care that belongs on this list is limiting the intake of stimulants, such as caffeine, and processed sugar, omnipresent substances in so much of what we consume and well known for substantially contributing to anxiety, stress, and mood dysregulation. That momentary joy of a candy bar or the quick jolt from a caffeinated beverage takes a toll on our sense of well-being in the long run. Eliminating such habits are well worth the effort if one wants to reduce stress and anxiety.[35]

It may go without saying that the overuse of alcohol and recreational substances are known contributors to anxiety, stress and depression.[36] That said, it cannot be emphasized enough how important it is to keep track of one's intake of such chemicals, and to recognize the long term deleterious effects. Even casual users may not recognize their actual level of consumption, and the impact that it may have on their well-being. Abstinence from all mind-altering substances is the only sure way to be certain that one is not being negatively affected by their use, and there is no downside, unless the user has developed a habit without recognizing it as such, which would certainly contribute to serious negative mental and emotional effects.[37]

Conclusion

As stated in the aforementioned IACP document, Critical Incident Stress Management, members of law enforcement agencies experience extreme traumatic events for which no amount of training can properly prepare them. All too often individual coping strategies that are used to deal with normal levels of stress are not adequate to help police personnel properly manage extreme traumatic stressors such as the ones experienced in a law enforcement critical incident. This inability to properly cope with such stressors can lead to critical incident stress reactions that are highly negative to the individual.

Our nation's law enforcement agencies need to rigorously adopt and promote stress reduction strategies, such as those presented here, and to increase awareness of these issues with their ranks.

ENDNOTES

1. IL Criminal Justice Info Authority, 2022.
2. Craddock & Telesco, 2022.
3. FBI, 2021.
4. CDC, 2021.
5. IL Criminal Justice Info Authority, 2022.
6. American Psychiatric Assn, 2022.
7. Craddock & Telesco, 2022.
8. IL Criminal Justice Info Authority, 2022.
9. American Psychological Assn, 2023.
10. IL Criminal Justice Info Authority, 2022.
11. American Psychiatric Assn, 2021.
12. Andrew, et al, 2011.
13. W.H.O., 2021.
14. Pathways Psych. Services, n.d.
15. IL Criminal Justice Info Authority, 2022.
16. NIMH, 2022.
17. Mayo Clinic 2023.
18. Andrew, et al, 2011.
19. IACP, 2011.
20. Quay, 2012.
21. Robinson, 2019.
22. NY Dept. of Environmental Conservation, n.d.
23. Britannica, 2022.
24. NY Times, 1975.
25. Baklouti, 2023.
26. Sassos, 2023.
27. Harvard, 2023.
28. McLean, 2023.
29. Wei, 2021.
30. WebMD, 2021.
31. Johnson & Wright, 2022.
32. Mayo Clinic, 2024.
33. Goldman, 2017.
34. Gradff-Radford, 2021.
35. Cassata, 2023.
36. Guarnotta, 2022.
37. Bernstein, et al, 2015.

REFERENCES

American Psychiatric Association, 2021, What are anxiety disorders? Retrieved from https://www.psychiatry.org/patients-families/anxiety-disorders/what-are-anxiety-disorders

American Psychological Association, 2023, Anxiety. Retrieved from https://www.apa.org/topics/anxiety

American Psychological Assn, 2022, Stress in America. Retrieved from https://www.apa.org/news/press/releases/stress/2022/concerned-future-inflation

Andrew, M., Burchfiel, C., Charles, L., Fekeduledgn, D, Hartley, T., Ma, C., Violanti, J., Am J Crim Justice. 2016 Dec; 41(4): 645–662. Retrieved from https://www.ncbi.nlm.nih.gov/pmc/articles/PMC5330309/

Baklouti, S., Fekih-Romdhane, F., Guelmami, N., Bonsaksen, T., Baklouti, H., Aloui, A., Masmoudi, L., Souissi, N., & Jarraya, M. (2023). The effect of web-based Hatha yoga on psychological distress and sleep quality in older adults: A randomized controlled trial. Complementary Therapies in Clinical Practice, 50, 101715. *Science Direct.* Retrieved from https://doi.org/10.1016/j.ctcp.2022.101715

Bernstein, J., et al, Changes in health outcomes as a function of abstinence and reduction in illicit psychoactive drug use: A prospective study in primary care. Retrieved from: https://www.ncbi.nlm.nih.gov/pmc/articles/PMC4521992/

Britannica, 2022 Hatha Yoga. Retrieved from https://www.britannica.com/topic/Hatha-Yoga

Cassata,C., 2023, The Experts Agree: What You Eat Can Directly Impact Stress and Anxiety. Retrieved from https://www.verywellmind.com/what-you-eat-can-have-an-effect-on-your-overall-mental-well-being-5209290

CDC, 2021, Suicides Among First Responders: A Call to Action, Retrieved from https://blogs.cdc.gov/niosh-science-blog/2021/04/06/suicides-first-responders/

Craddock T., Telesco, G., 2022, Police Stress and Deleterious Outcomes: Efforts Towards Improving Police Mental Health. Retrieved from https://www.ncbi.nlm.nih.gov/pmc/articles/PMC8575544/

Guarnotta, E., 2023, The Connection Between Stress and Substance Abuse. Retrieved from https://oxfordtreatment.com/substance-abuse/co-occurring-disorders/stress/

IL Criminal Justice Information Authority, 2022, Research suggests that police officers exhibit higher rates of PTSD than the general population…Retrieved from https://icjia.illinois.gov/researchhub/articles/understanding-police-officer-stress-a-review-of-the-literature

FBI Law Enforcement Bulletin, 2021, Law Enforcement Officers Killed in the Line of Duty Statistics for 2021. Retrieved from https://leb.fbi.gov/bulletin-highlights/additional-highlights/crime-data-law-enforcement-officers-killed-in-the-line-of-duty-statistics-for-2021

Goldman, J., 2017, The-Humming-Effect, Retrieved from https://www.simonandschuster.com/books/The-Humming-Effect/Jonathan-Goldman/9781620554845

Graff-Radford, M., 2021, Humming your way to relaxation. Retrieved from https://connect.mayoclinic.org/blog/living-with-mild-cognitive-impairment-mci/newsfeed-post/humming-your-way-to-relaxation/

Harvard, 2023, Mindfulness, Retrieved from https://hr.harvard.edu/mindfulness

International Association of Chiefs of Police, 2011, National Law Enforcement Policy Center, Critical Incident Stress Management Concepts and Issues. Retrieved from https://www.theiacp.org/sites/default/files/all/c/CriticalIncidentStressPaper.pdf

Johnson, J., Wright, S., 2022, The Benefits of Relaxation and Relaxation Techniques to Try. Retrieved from https://psychcentral.com/lib/relaxation-make-time-and-take-time-for-self-care

Mayo Clinic, 2023, Depression (major depressive disorder), Retrieved from https://www.mayoclinic.org/diseases-conditions/depression/symptoms-causes/syc-20356007

Mayo Clinic Staff, 2024, Relaxation techniques: Try these steps to lower stress. Retrieved from https://www.mayoclinic.org/healthy-lifestyle/stress-management/in-depth/relaxation-technique/art-20045368

McLean Hospital, 2023, Serenity Now: Everything You Need to Know About Mindfulness, retrieved from https://www.mcleanhospital.org/essential/mindfulness

National Institute of Mental Health [NIMH], 2022, Prevalence of any anxiety disorder among adults. Retrieved from https://www.nimh.nih.gov/health/statistics/any-anxiety-disorder

National Institute of Mental Health [NIMH], 2022, Major depression, Retrieved from https://www.nimh.nih.gov/health/statistics/major-depression

New York State Department of Environmental Conservation [DEC], n.d., Immerse yourself in a forest for better health. Retrieved from https://www.dec.ny.gov/lands/90720

New York Times, 1975, India evaluating effects of yoga, retrieved from https://www.nytimes.com/1975/11/30/archives/india-evaluating-effects-of-yoga-researchers-find-practice-relieves.html

Office of Disease Prevention and Health Promotion, 2023, Managing stress, Retrieved from https://health.gov/myhealthfinder/health-conditions/heart-health/manage-stress

Pathways Psychology Services, n.d., Climb every mountain and find your path. Retrieved from http://www.pathwayspsychologicalservices.com/

Quay, J, 2012, Kurt Hahn: Inspirational, visionary, outdoor and experiential educator, Australian Journal of Outdoor Education

Robinson, S., 2019, Doctors urged to prescribe woodland walks for mental health problems. Retrieved from https://www.news-medical.net/news/20190610/Doctors-urged-to-prescribe-woodland-walks-for-mental-health-problems.

Sassos, S., 2023, A Complete Guide to Yoga for Beginners. Retrieved from https://www.goodhousekeeping.com/health/fitness/a42396941/yoga-for-beginners/

WebMD, 2021, Mental benefits of walking. Retrieved from https://www.webmd.com/fitness-exercise/mental-benefits-of-walking

Wei, 2021, 6 Surprising Health Benefits of Walking Through a Forest Retrieved from https://www.psychologytoday.com/us/blog/urban-survival/202108/6-surprising-health-benefits-walking-through-forest

World Health Organization [WHO], 2021, Stress. Retrieved from https://www.who.int/news-room/questions-and-answers/item/stress#

www.ingramcontent.com/pod-product-compliance
Lightning Source LLC
LaVergne TN
LVHW022052200926
848481LV00003B/875
* 9 7 9 8 3 8 5 1 2 5 6 5 4 *